Simple Crochet Doily Guide For Beginners

Mia O. Murphy

Introduction

Welcome to this book, a comprehensive resource to help you master the art of crocheting beautiful doilies. Whether you're new to crochet or looking to expand your skills, this guide will provide you with step-by-step instructions and patterns to create stunning doilies that will add an elegant touch to your home decor.

In the beginning, we'll familiarize ourselves with the common abbreviations used in crochet patterns. Understanding these abbreviations will make following the instructions much easier and allow you to dive into the world of doily making with confidence.

We'll start our journey by exploring the basic center patterns for doilies. These patterns serve as the foundation for your doily and will set the stage for the intricate designs to come. You'll learn various techniques and stitches to create captivating centerpieces that form the heart of your doily.

Once you've mastered the basics, we'll move on to ruffled doilies. These doilies feature delicate, frilly edges that add a touch of whimsy and charm to your creations. You'll learn different stitch patterns and techniques to achieve the desired ruffled effect, allowing you to create doilies that stand out and make a statement.

After completing your doilies, you may want to enhance their shape and structure by starching them. Starching helps to preserve the intricate details of your work and gives your doilies a crisp, polished look. We'll provide you with easy-to-follow directions for starching your doilies, ensuring they maintain their beauty for years to come.

Whether you're crocheting doilies for personal use, gifting them to loved ones, or even considering selling your creations, this guide will equip you with the necessary skills and knowledge to create stunning doilies that showcase your talent and creativity.

So, grab your crochet hook and yarn, and let's embark on a journey of creating beautiful, intricate doilies. Get ready to add a touch of elegance and artistry to your home with this book.

Contents

Abbreviations

St - stitch
sl st - slip stitch
Ch - chain
Lp - loop
Hk - hook
Sc - single crochet Dc - double crochet Hdc - half double crochet Trc
- treble crochet Dtrc - double treble crochet Yo - yarn over
Tog - together
Inc - increase
Dec - decrease
Sk - skip
Basic Centers For:

Here is the very newest, the very smartest scheme for delightful table
settings. A set of doilies with identical centers in different gay flower
borders that will add a decorator's touch to your luncheon table. We

have designed the above four doilies with just that idea in mind. All four designs fit either of the two basic centers.

TABLE ENSEMBLE SUGGESTIONS: Why not make the other doilies in this book for a service of eight, all in White and bright flower colors?

BASIC CENTER #1

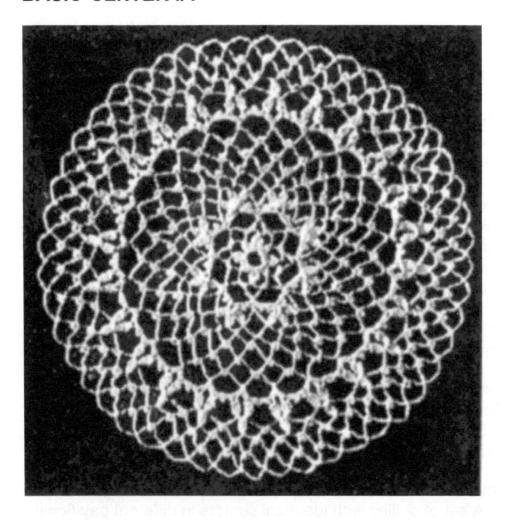

With White ch 12, join to form a ring, ch 4, work 3 tr c in ring keeping last loop of each tr c on hook, thread over and work off all loops at one time, * ch 6, 4 d c in ring, keeping last loop of each d c on hook, thread over and work off all loops at one time (d c cluster st), ch 6, 4 tr c in ring, keeping last loop of each tr c on hook, thread over and work off all loops at one time (4 tr c cluster st), repeat from * twice, ch 6, d c cluster st in ring, ch 2, tr c in 1st cluster st (this brings thread in position for next row).

2nd Row—3 s c over tr c, * ch 7, 3 s c in next loop, repeat from * all around, ending row with ch 3, d c in tr c.

3rd Row—* Ch 9, s c in next loop, repeat from * all around.
4th Row—Over next loop work 3 s c, * ch 3, 3 s c, repeat from * twice, repeat from beginning all around, join.

5th Row—Ch 5, skip 1 ch 3 loop, 3-3 tr c cluster sts with ch 5 between each cluster st in next loop, ch 5, skip 5 s c, s c in space between next 2 s c, repeat from beginning all around in same manner ending row after last cluster st with d tr c (3 times over needle) in joining.

6th Row—Ch 4, ** tr c in next cluster st, * ch 7, s c in next loop, repeat from * once, ch 7, tr c in next cluster st, repeat from ** 6 times, tr c in next cluster st, * ch 7, s c in next loop, repeat from * once, ch 3, tr c in tr c.

7th Row—Ch 3, s c over tr c, * ch 9, s c, ch 3, s c in next loop, repeat from * all around, ending row with ch 4, tr tr c (4 times over needle) in tr c.

8th and 9th Rows—Ch 3, s c over same loop, * ch 9, s c, ch 3, s c in next large loop, repeat from * all around ending each row with ch 4, tr tr c in tr tr c.

10th Row—Ch 10, s c in next loop, repeat from beginning all around ending row with sl st in tr tr c.
11th Row—Same as 4th row.

12th Row—Sl st to 1st ch 3, ch 4, 2 tr c cluster st in same space, * ch 10, skip
1 ch 3 loop, 1-3 tr c cluster st in each of the next 2 ch 3 loops with ch 1 between, repeat from * all around ending row with ch 10, 3 tr c cluster st in last ch 3 loop, ch 1, join in 1st cluster st.

13th Row—Ch 4, 2 tr c cluster st in same space, * ch 6, s c, ch 3, s c in next loop, ch 6, 1-3 tr c cluster st in ch 1 between next 2 cluster sts, repeat from * all around in the same manner ending row with ch 3, tr c in 1st cluster st.

14th Row—Work in the same manner as 8th row ending row with ch 4, tr tr c in tr c.
15th Row—Same as last row ending row with ch 4, tr tr c in tr tr c.

16th Row—Ch 8, s c in next loop, repeat from beginning all around ending row with sl st in tr tr c (48 loops).

BASIC CENTER #2

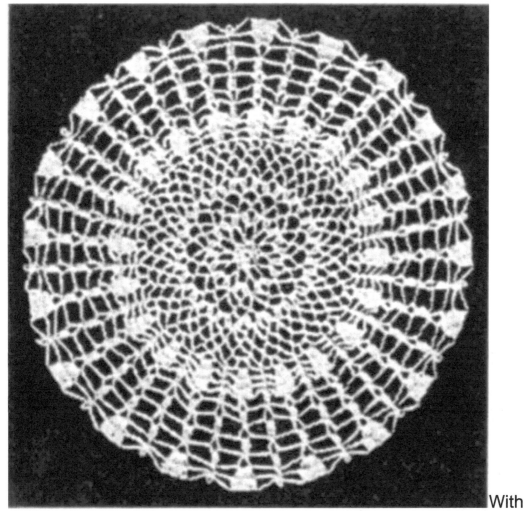

With White ch 5, join to form a ring, ch 3 and work 9 d c in ring, join in 3rd st of ch.

2nd Row—* Ch 7, s c in next d c, repeat from * all around ending row with ch 2, d tr c in same space as beginning (this brings thread in position for next row).

3rd Row—Ch 3, 1 d c, ch 3, 2 d c in same space, * 2 d c, ch 3, 2 d c (shell) in next loop, repeat from * all around, join.

4th Row—* Ch 5, s c in center of next shell, ch 5, s c between shells, repeat from * all around, ending the row with ch 2, d c in the same space as beginning.

5th Row—* Ch 5, s c in next loop, repeat from * all around, ending row with ch 2, d c in d c.
6th Row—Same as 3rd row.
7th Row—Same as 4th row.
8th and 9th Rows—Same as 5th row.

10th Row—Ch 6, d c in same space, * ch 3, s c in next loop, ch 3, 1 d c, ch 3, 1 d c in next loop, repeat from * all around ending row with ch 3, s c in next loop, ch 3, join in 3rd st of ch.

11th Row—Sl st into loop, ch 3, 2 d c in same space, * ch 4, s c in next s c, ch
4, skip 1 loop, 3 d c in next loop, repeat from * all around ending row with ch 4, s c in next s c, ch 4, join.

12th Row—Ch 3, d c in same space, 1 d c in next d c, 2 d c in next d c, * ch 4, s c in next sc, ch 4, 2 d c in next d c, 1 d c in next d c, 2 d c in next d c, repeat from * all around ending row with ch 4, s c in next s c, ch 4, join.

13th Row—Ch 3, 1 d c in each of the next 4 d c, * ch 5, s c in next 5 c, ch 5, 1 d c in each of the next 5 d c, repeat from * all around ending row with ch 5, s c in next s c, ch 5, join.

14th Row—Sl st to center d c of group, ch 6, d c in same space, * ch 5, cluster st in next s c (cluster st: 3 d c in same space keeping last loop of each d c on hook, thread over and pull through all loops at one time), ch 5, 1 d c, ch 3, 1 d c (shell) in center d c of next d c group, repeat from * all around, ending row to correspond, ch 5, join in 3rd st of ch.

15th Row—Sl st into loop, ch 3 (counts as part of 1st cluster st) cluster st in same space, * ch 5, 1 d c, ch 3, 1 d c in next cluster st, ch 5, cluster st in center of next shell, repeat from * all around, ending row to correspond, ch 5, join.

16th Row—Ch 6, d c in same space, * ch 5, cluster st in center of next shell, ch 5, shell in next cluster st, repeat from * all around, ending row to correspond, ch 5, join.

17th Row—Same as 15th row but working 6 chs in each loop before and after each cluster st.
18th Row—Same as 16th row but having 6 chs in each loop before and after each cluster st.

19th Row—Sl st into loop, ch 3, 4 d c in same space, ch 6, * s c in next cluster st, ch 6, 5 d c in center of next shell, ch 6, repeat from * all around, ending row to correspond.

20th Row—Ch 3, d c in same space, 1 d c in each of the next 3 d c, 2 d c in next d c, * ch 6, sl st in next s c, ch 3, sl st in same space for picot, ch 6, 2 d c in next d c, 1 d c in each of the next 3 d c, 2 d c in next d c, repeat from * all around, ending row to correspond, join.
Spider Web Doily

This doily may be made with any of the American Thread Company products listed on the next page:

Material	Quantity	Approx. Size of Doily	Size of Needle
"GEM" Crochet Cotton Article 35, Size 30 or 50	1 Ball White	11 Inches	Steel 12
or			
"PURITAN" Crochet Cotton Article 40	1 Ball White	13 "	" 7
or			
"DE LUXE" Crochet Cotton Article 346	1 Ball White	13 "	" 7
or			
"STAR" Tatting Cotton Article 25	2 Balls White	9 "	" 13
or			
"STAR" Crochet Cotton Article 20, Size 30 or 50	1 Ball White	11 "	" 12
or			
"STAR" Crochet Cotton Article 30, Size 30 or 50	2 Balls White	11 "	" 12
or			
"STAR" Pearl Cotton Article 90, Size 5	3 Balls White	13 "	" 7
or			
"SILLATEEN SANSIL" Article 102	2 Balls White	12 "	" 10

Ch 2,
8 s c in 2nd st from hook, join in 1st s c.
2nd Row—Ch 1 and work 2 s c in each s c (16 s c), join.
3rd Row—Working in s c increase in every other s c, join.
4th Row—Increase in every 3rd s c, join.
5th Row—Increase in every 4th s c (40 s c), join.

6th Row—Ch 5, d c in same space, * skip 1 s c, 1 d c, ch 2, 1 d c (shell) in next s c, repeat from * all around, ending row with skip 1 s c,

9

join in 3rd st of ch.

7th Row—Sl st into shell, ch 5, d c in same space, * 1 d c, ch 2, 1 d c (shell) in center of next shell, repeat from * all around, join in 3rd st of ch.

8th Row—Sl st into shell, ch 7 and work the same as the last row but working 1 d c, ch 4, 1 d c in the center of each shell.

9th Row—Sl st into shell, ch 8 and work same as last row but working 1 d c, ch 5, 1 d c in center of each shell.

10th Row—* Ch 6, s c in center of next shell, ch 6, s c between next 2 d c, repeat from * all around ending row with ch 3, d c in same space as beginning (this brings thread in position for next row).

11th, 12th, 13th and 14th Rows—Work ch 6 loops all around ending each row with ch 3, d c in d c (40 loops in each row).

15th Row—Ch 9, 3 s c in next loop, * ch 5, tr c in next loop, ch 5, 3 s c in next loop, repeat from * all around, ch 5, join in 4th st of ch.

16th Row—Ch 1, s c in same space, * s c in 1st st of ch of next loop, ch 5, tr c in center s c of next s c group, ch 5, 1 s c in last st of ch of next loop, 1 s c in tr c, repeat from * all around, ending row with s c in 1st st of ch of next loop, ch 5, tr c in center s c of next s c group, ch 5, s c in last st of ch of next loop, join.

17th Row—Ch 1, s c in same space, 1 s c in next s c, * ch 6, tr c in next tr c, ch 6, 1 s c in each of the next 3 s c, repeat from * all around, ending row with ch 6, tr c in tr c, ch 6, s c in next s c, join in 1st s c.

18th Row—Ch 11, * 1 s c in last st of ch of next loop, 1 sc in tr c, 1 sc in 1st st of ch of next loop, ch 7, tr c in center s c of next s c group, ch 7, repeat from * all around, ending row to correspond, join in 4th st of ch.

19th Row—Ch 11, * 1 s c in each of the next 3 s c, ch 7, tr c in next tr c, ch 7, repeat from * all around, ending row to correspond, join in 4th st of ch.

20th Row—Same as 16th row but having 8 chs in each loop.

21st Row—Same as 17th row but having 8 chs in each loop.

22nd Row—Ch 12 and work same as 18th row but having 8 chs in each loop.

23rd Row—Ch 13 and work same as 19th row having 9 chs in each loop.

24th Row—Same as 16th row but having 9 chs in each loop.

25th Row—Same as 17th row but having 10 chs in each loop.

26th Row—Ch 14 and work same as 18th row but having 10 chs in each loop.

Continued from Page 7

27th Row—Ch 7, tr c in same space, * ch 10, 1 s c in each of the next 3 s c, ch

10, tr c in next tr c, ch 10, 1 s c in each of the next 3 s c, ch 10, 1 tr c, ch 3, 1 tr c in next tr c, repeat from * all around, ending row with ch 10, 1 s c in each of the next 3 s c, ch 10, tr c in next tr c, ch 10, 1 s c in each of the next 3 s c, ch 10, join in 4th st of ch.

28th Row—Sl st into loop, ch 4, 11 tr c in same loop, * ch 8, 1 tr c in center s c of next s c group, ch 8, s c in last st of ch of next loop, s c in next tr c, s c in

1st st of ch of next loop, ch 8, tr c in center s c of next s c group, ch 8, skip 1 loop, 12 tr c in next loop, repeat from * all around, ending row to correspond, join.

29th Row—Ch 4, ** tr c in next tr c, * ch 3, 1 tr c in each of the next 2 tr c, repeat from * 4 times, ch 9, tr c in next tr c, ch 9, 1 s c in each of the next 3 s c, ch 9, tr c in next tr c, ch 9, 1 tr c in next tr c, repeat from ** all around, ending row to correspond, join.

30th Row—Sl st into loop, ch 11, s c in next loop, * ch 7, tr c in next loop, ch 7, s c in next loop, ch 7, tr c in next loop, ch 8, 1 s c in last st of ch of next loop, s c in next tr c, s c in 1st st of ch of next loop, ch 8, tr c in center s c of next s c group, ch 8, s c in last st of ch of next loop, s c in next tr c, s c in 1st st of ch of next loop, ch 8, skip 1 loop, tr c in next ch 3 loop, ch 7, s c in next loop, repeat from * all around ending row to correspond and joining last ch 8 loop in 4th st of ch.

31st Row—Ch 1, s c in same space, 1 s c in 1st st of ch of next loop, ** ch 7, tr c in next s c, ch 7, s c in last st of ch of next loop, s c in next tr c, s c in 1st st of ch of next loop, repeat from * once, * ch 8, tr c in center s c of next s c group, ch 8, s c in last st of ch of next loop, s c in next tr c, s c in 1st st of ch of next loop, repeat from * once, repeat from ** all around in the same manner ending row to correspond, join.

32nd Row—Ch 12, * s c in last st of ch of next loop, s c in tr c, s c in 1st st of next loop, ch 8, tr c in center s c of next s c group, ch 8, repeat from * all around ending row to correspond and joining last ch 8 in 4th st of ch 12.

33rd Row—Sl st to center of loop, * ch 9, sl st in 4th st from hook for picot, ch s, s c in next loop, repeat from * all around, join, break

thread. Rose Ruffle Doily

This doily may be made with any of the American Thread Company products listed on next page:

Material	Quantity	Approx. Size of Doily	Size of Needle
"GEM" Crochet Cotton Article 35, Size 30	1 Ball White 1 Ball Light Pink 1 Ball Dark Pink 1 Ball Nile Green	9 Inches	Steel 12
or			
"STAR" Tatting Cotton Article 25	2 Balls White 2 Balls Light Pink 1 Ball Dark Pink 1 Ball Nile Green	7 "	" 13
or			
"STAR" Crochet Cotton Article 20, Size 30	1 Ball White 1 Ball Light Pink 1 Ball Dark Pink 1 Ball Nile Green	9 "	" 12
or			
"STAR" Crochet Cotton Article 30, Size 30	2 Balls White 2 Balls Light Pink 1 Ball Dark Pink 1 Ball Nile Green	9 "	" 12

ROSE—With Dark Pink ch 5, join to form a ring, ch 6, d c in ring, * ch 3, d c in ring, repeat from * twice, ch 3, join in 3rd st of ch.

2nd Row—1 s c, 5 d c, 1 s c over each ch 3 loop, join.
3rd Row—* Ch 5, s c between next 2 petals in back of work, repeat from * 4 times.
4th Row—Ch 1 and over each loop work 1 s c, 7 d c, 1 s c, join.
5th Row—* Ch 6, s c in back of work between next 2 petals, repeat from * 4 times.
6th Row—Ch 1 and over each loop work 1 s c, 9 d c, 1 s c, join, break thread.

7th Row—Attach Green in same space, * ch 7, s c in 2nd st from hook, 1 s d c in each of the next 2 sts of ch (s d c: thread over hook, insert in st, pull through, thread over and pull through all loops at one time), 1 d c in each of the next 3 sts of ch, s c in same space between petals, ch 6, s c in back of work between next 2 petals, repeat from * all around (5 leaves) ch 6, join.

8th Row—Work 5 s c up side of next leaf, 3 s c in point of leaf, 5 s c down other side of same leaf, 8 s c over next ch 6 loop, repeat from beginning 4 times, break thread.

9th Row—Start Petal: Attach Light Pink in 1st s c of the 8 s c group between leaves, ch 3, d c in same space, 1 d c in each of the next 2 s c, 2 d c in each of the next 2 s c, 1 d c in each of the next 2 s c, 2 d c in next s c, ch 3, turn.

10th Row—2 d c in the same space, 1 d c in each of the next 10 d c, 3 d c in 3rd st of ch, ch 3, turn.
11th Row—Working in d c, increase 1 d c at each end and in each of the 2 center sts, ch 3 to turn each row (20 d c).
12th Row—Increase 1 d c at beginning and end of row (22 d c).
13th Row—Same as 11th row having 26 d c in row.
14th Row—Same as 12th row (28 d c).
15th Row—Increase 1 d c at each end and increase 1 d c in each of the 2 center sts (32 d c).
16th Row—Work even.
17th Row—Increase 1 d c at beginning and end of row. Repeat the last 2 rows once, then work 2 rows even.

22nd Row—Decrease in next 2 sts (to decrease: * thread over hook, insert in next st, pull through and work off 2 loops, repeat from * once, thread over and pull through all loops at one time), 1 d c in each of the next 31 d c, decrease in next 2 sts.
23rd Row—Decrease 1 d c at beginning and end of row, ch 1, turn.

24th Row—Skip 1 d c, s c in next d c, 1 s d c in each of the next 2 d c, 1 d c in each of the next 6 d c, 1 tr c in each of the next 12 d c, 1 d c in each of the next 6 d c, 1 s d c in each of the next 2 d c, s c in next st, break thread.

Attach thread in 1st s c of next s c group of 8th row and work another petal in the same manner, break thread. Work 3 more petals the same as the last petal, break thread.

Attach Dark Pink at the base of any petal and work a row of s c around each petal working 3 s c in the top of each corner of the petal, break thread.
Sew petals together from the 9th through the 16th row as illustrated.

LEAF: With Green ch 19, sl st in 2nd st from hook, 1 s c in each of the next 2 sts of ch, 1 s d c in each of the next 2 sts, 1 d c in each of the next 2 sts of ch, 1 tr c in each of the next 4 sts of ch, 1 d c in each of the next 2 sts, 1 s d c in each of the next 2 sts, 1 s c in each of the next 2 sts, 1 sl st in last st of ch, ch 1 and working on other side of ch, sl st in next st, 1 s c in each of the next 2 sts, 1 s d c in each of the next 2 sts, 1 d c in each of the next 2 sts, 1 tr c in each of the next 4 sts, 1 d c in each of the next 2 sts, 1 s d c in each of the next 2 sts, 1 s c in each of the next 2 sts, 1 sl st in next st.

2nd Row—Ch 1, 1 s c in each of the next 2 sts, 1 s d c in each of the next 3 sts, 1 d c in each of the next 8 sts, 1 s d c in each of the next 2 sts, 1 s c in each of the next 2 sts, 1 sl st in next st, ch 1, 1 s c in each of the next 2 sts, 1 s d c in each of the next 2 sts, 1 d c in each of the next 8 sts, 1 s d c in each of the next 2 sts, 1 s c in each of the next 2 sts, sl st in each of the next 2 sts, break thread leaving an end. Work 4 more leaves in the same manner and sew in space between petals picking up the back loop of sts only and sewing to the widest part of the leaf.
RUFFLE—Attach White in center of any petal, * ch 4, skip 1 st, s c in next st, repeat from * to within 3 sts of joining, skip 1 st, d c in next st keeping last loop of d c on hook, skip 1 st of same petal and 1 st on side of next leaf, d c in next st keeping last loop of d c on hook,

thread over and pull through all 3 loops at one time, * ch 4, skip 1 st, s c in next st, repeat from * around leaf to within 3 sts of joining on left hand side of leaf, skip 1 st, d c in next st keeping last loop of d c on hook, skip 1 st on leaf and 1 st on side of next petal, d c in next st keeping last loop of d c on hook, thread over and pull through all loops at one time, * ch 4, skip 1 st of petal, s c in next st, repeat from * all around in the same manner working between joinings same as on 1st leaf.

2nd Row—Sl st into loop, ch 6, s c in same loop, * ch 6, s c in next loop, ch
6, s c in next loop, ch 6, s c in same loop, repeat from * all around ending row with ch 3, d c in sl st (this brings thread in position for next row).

3rd Row—* Ch 6, s c in next loop, repeat from * all around, ending row with ch 3, d c in d c. Work 6 more rows same as last row, but ending last row with ch 6, s c in d c and having an even number of loops in the last row, break thread.

10th Row—Attach Dark Pink in any loop, ** ch 4, cluster st in next loop (cluster st: thread over hook, insert in space, pull through and work off 2 loops, * thread over hook, insert in same space, pull through and work off 2 loops, repeat from * once, thread over and pull through all loops at one time), ch 5, sl st in 3rd st from hook for picot, ch 2, cluster st in same loop, ch 4, s c in next loop, repeat from ** all around, ch 4, join, break thread. Grape Doily

These doilies may be made with any of the American Thread Company products listed on the next page:

Material for each Doily	Quantity	Approx. Size of Doily	Size of Needle
"GEM" Crochet Cotton Article 35	1 Ball Shaded Lavenders 1 Ball White 1 Ball Green	9 Inches	Steel 12
or			
"PURITAN" Crochet Cotton Article 40	1 Ball Shaded Lavenders 1 Ball White 1 Ball Green	11 "	" 7
or			
"DE LUXE" Crochet Cotton Article 346	1 Ball Shaded Lavenders 1 Ball White 1 Ball Green	11 "	" 7
or			
"STAR" Tatting Cotton Article 25	2 Balls Shaded Lavenders 2 Balls White 2 Balls Green	7 "	" 13
or			
"STAR" Crochet Cotton Article 20, Size 30	1 Ball Shaded Lavenders 1 Ball White 1 Ball Green	9 "	" 12
or			
"STAR" Crochet Cotton Article 30, Size 30	2 Balls Shaded Lavenders 2 Balls White 2 Balls Green	9 "	" 12
or			
"STAR" Pearl Cotton Article 90, Size 5	3 Balls Shaded Lavenders 2 Balls White 3 Balls Green	11 "	" 7
or			
"SILLATEEN SANSIL" Article 102	2 Balls Shaded Lavenders 2 Balls White 2 Balls Green	10 "	" 10

SMALL LEAF—With Green ch 4, 3 s c in 2nd st from hook, 5 d c in next st of ch, 3 s c in next st, ch 1 to turn all rows.

2nd Row—Working in s c work 3 s c in 1st and last s c. Work 1 row even.

4th Row—Increase 1 s c in 1st and last s c. Work 1 row even.

6th and 7th rows—2 s c in 1st s c, 1 s c in each remaining s c.

8th row—same as 4th row.

9th Row—2 s c in 1st s c, 1 s c in each of the next 17 s c, 2 s c in next s c.

10th Row—3 s c in 1st s c, 1 s c in each of the next 15 s c, 2 s c in last s c.

11th and 12th Rows—Increase 2 s c in 1st s c and 1 s c in last s c.

13th Row—3 s c in 1st s c, 1 s c in each of the next 21 s c.

14th Row—Skip 1 s c, 1 s c in each of the next 15 s c, 2 s c in next s c.

15th Row—2 s c in 1st s c, 1 s c in each of the next 13 s c, 2 s c in next s c.

16th Row—Increase 1 s c in 1st s c.

Next 3 Rows—Decrease 1 st in 1st and last s c (to decrease: * insert hook in next st, pull loop through, repeat from *, thread over and work off all loops at one time).

20th Row—Skip 1 st, decrease in next 2 sts, 1 s c in each of the next 6 s c, decrease in next 2 sts.

21st Row—Skip 1 st, decrease in next 2 sts, 1 s c in each of the next 3 s c, decrease in next 2 sts. Work 1 row even.

23rd Row—* Decrease in next 2 sts, repeat from * once.

24th Row—Decrease in 1st 2 sts, break thread. Work 3 more leaves in same manner.

LARGE LEAF: With Green work same as 1st 19 rows of small leaf.

20th Row—Work even.

21st Row—Decrease 1 st at the beginning and end of row. Repeat the last 2 rows twice.

26th Row—Decrease in 1st 2 sts.

27th Row—Decrease in last 2 sts. Repeat the last 2 rows.

30th Row—Decrease in 1st 2 sts, break thread. Work 3 more leaves in same manner.

GRAPE: With Shaded Lavenders ch 5, join to form a ring, ch 1 and work 8 s c in ring, join.

2nd Row—Ch 1, 2 s c in each s c. Do not join or turn this or following rows.

3rd Row—1 s c in 1st s c, 2 s c in next s c, repeat from beginning all around.

4th Row—Increase in every 3rd st (32 s c), join, break thread.

Work 13 more grapes in the same manner, always increasing and joining in the last row as illustrated. Work 3 more bunches of grapes in the same manner.

IF YOU ARE MAKING BASIC DOILY No. 1 SHOWN ON Page 4 - With White 5 s c in next loop, ch 1, join to 6th s c of 4th grape to right of 2nd joining (to join: sl loop off hook, insert in st, pull loop through) ch 1, 4 s c in same loop, * 5 s c in next loop, ch 1, join to center s c between joinings of next grape, ch 1, 4 s c in same space, repeat from * once, 6 s c in next loop, ch 1, join to 5th s c from left of joining of next grape, ch 1, 3 s c in same loop, 2 s c in next loop, ch 1, skip 4 s c of same grape, join in next st, ch 1, 7 s c in same loop, 9 s c in next loop, 7 s c in next loop, ch 1, join to 1st point on side of large leaf as illustrated, ch 1, 2 s c in same loop, 7 s c in next loop, ch 1, join to next point, ch 1, 2 s c in same loop, 9 s c in next loop, 7 s c in next loop, ch 1, with 2 large points on side of small leaf to the right, join to last st of 1st row, ch 1, 2 s c in same loop, 4 s c in next loop, ch 1, join to last st of 3rd row, ch 1, 5 s c in same loop, 9 s c in next loop, repeat from beginning all around, join, break thread. Sew point of small leaf to center st of large leaf and opposite point of same leaf to grape, sew top of large leaf to grape as illustrated.

Stem—Attach Green in same space as 1st point of large leaf, ch 2, s c in 2nd st from hook, * ch 1, s c in s c, repeat from * 8 times or until the stem is long enough to reach the 7th st to the left of the joining of center grape at end, join, break thread. Attach Green in 5th st of 1st large point of next large leaf and work a stem of 8 s c or long enough to reach the 6th st to left of joining of center grape at end, join, break thread. Work 2 more stems in the same manner.

IF YOU ARE MAKING BASIC CENTER No. 2 SHOWN ON Page 6 - Work 19 rows of basic center, ch 4, * join to 10th s c to left of 2nd joining of 4th grape, ch 1, d c in same space on center, 1 d c in each of the next 4 d c, ch 1, join to 5th s c to left of joining of next grape, ch 1, d c in same space on center, ch 6, sl st in next s c, ch 3, sl st in same space for picot, ch 6, d c in next d c, ch 1, join to 5th s c of next grape to right of joining, ch 1, d c in same space on center, 1 d c in each of the next 4 d c, ch 1, join to 5th s c to left of joining of next grape, ch 1, d c in same space on center, ch 6, sl st in next s c, ch 3, sl st in same space for picot, ch 6, 2 d c in next d c, 1 d c in each of the next 2 d c, join to 1st large point on side of large leaf as illustrated, d c in next d c on center, 2 d c in next d c, join to next point of same leaf, ch 6, sl st in next s c, ch 3 picot, ch 6, 2 d c in next d c, 1 d c in each of the next 3 d c, 2 d c in next d c, with 2 large points of small leaf to the left, join to 1st st of 1st row, ch 6, sl st in next s c, ch 3 picot, ch 6, d c in next d c, ch 1, join to last st of 4th row of same leaf, ch 1, d c in same space on center, 1 d c in each of the next 3 d c, 2 d c in next d c, ch 6, sl st in next s c, ch 3 picot, ch 6, d c in next d c, ch 1, repeat from * all around, join, break thread.

Sew top of large leaf to grape, sew large point of small leaf to center st of large leaf, sew large point on opposite side of leaf to grape as illustrated. Stem—Attach Green in 3rd st of 1st point of large leaf, ch 2, s c in 2nd st from hook, * ch 1, s c in s c, repeat from * 6 times, join to 3rd st from joining of center grape, as illustrated, break thread. Work 3 more stems.

Violet Doilies

These doilies may be made with any of the American Thread
Company products listed below:

Material for each Doily	Quantity	Approx. Size of Doily	Size of Needle
"GEM" Crochet Cotton Article 35, Size 30	1 Ball Shaded Lavenders 1 Ball Yellow 1 Ball Green 1 Ball White	9 inches	Steel 12
or			
"PURITAN" Crochet Cotton " Article 40		11 "	" 7
or			
"DE LUXE" Crochet Cotton " Article 346		11 "	" 7
or			
"STAR" Crochet Cotton Article 20, Size 30	"	9 "	" 12
or			
"STAR" Crochet Cotton Article 30, Size 30	"	9 "	" 12
or			
"SILLATEEN SANSIL" Article 102	"	10 "	" 10
or			
"STAR" Tatting Cotton Article 25	2 Balls Shaded Lavenders 2 Balls White 1 Ball Green 1 Ball Yellow	7 "	" 13
or			
"STAR" Pearl Cotton Article 90, Size 5	"	11 "	" 7

VIOLET: With Yellow ch 6, join to form a ring, ch 1 and work 10 s c in ring, join, break thread.
2nd Row—Attach Shaded Lavenders, * 2 s c in each of the next 2 s c of 1st row, ch 1 to turn all rows.

3rd Row—1 s c in each s c.

4th Row—Increase 1 s c at beginning and end of row (6 s c). Work 1 row even.

6th and 7th Rows—Decrease 1 s c at beginning of each row, ch 2, turn.

8th Row—1 d c in each of the next 3 s c leaving last loop of each d c on hook, thread over and pull through all loops at one time, ch 3, sl st in base of same row, sl st in each row down side of petal, repeat from * until there are 5 petals, join in the base of the 1st petal, break thread. Work 2nd violet in the same manner joining the tip of 1 petal to the tip of any petal of 1st violet. To join: ch 2, sl st in tip of previous violet, ch 2, sl st in same space on violet being made. Work 16 more violets joining to the petals of the previous violet leaving 1 petal free at lower edge and 2 petals free at top between joinings.

IF YOU ARE MAKING BASIC CENTER No. 1 SHOWN ON Page 4 - With White work a row of 9 ch loops all around increasing in every 8th loop on center (54 loops).

Attach Green in loop, 4 s c over same loop, ch 1 and with the single petals next to center, s c in single free petal of violet, ch 1, 4 s c over same loop on center, * 3 s c over next loop, ch 5, sl st in 7th row on left hand side of same petal, ch 1, skip 1 st of ch, 1 s c in each of the next 4 sts of ch, 2 s c in same loop on center, ch 7, sl st in 7th row of next petal of same flower to right of joining, ch 1, skip 1 st of ch, 1 s c in each of the next 6 sts, 3 s c over same loop on center, 3 s c over next loop, ch 7, sl st in 7th row to left of joining of next violet, ch 1, skip 1 st of ch, 1 s c in each of the next 6 sts, 2 s c over same loop on center, ch 5, sl st in 7th row on right hand side of next petal of same flower, ch 1, skip 1 st of ch, 1 s c in each of the next 4 sts, 4 s c over same loop, 4 s c over next loop, ch 1, s c in tip of same petal, ch 1, 4 s c over same loop on center, repeat from * in the same manner until all flowers are IF YOU ARE MAKING BASIC CENTER No. 2

SHOWN ON Page 6 - Work violets same as for Basic Center No. 1 but working 5 groups of 3 violets each and using ch 1 between joinings.

Attach Green in 1st d c of any d c group on center, s c in same space, 1 s c in each of the next 3 d c, ch 4, sl st in last s c for picot, 1 s c in each of the next 3 d c, holding violets with 2 free petals next to center, ** ch 1, sl st in tip of 1st free petal of 1st violet of any 3 violet group, ch 1, sl st in same s c on center, ch 5, thread over hook twice, insert in 5th st from hook, pull through, thread over and work off 2 loops twice, thread over hook twice, insert in same space, pull through, thread over and work off 2 loops twice, thread over and pull through remaining loops at one time (a rice st), ch 4, sl st in top of rice st for picot, ch 5, rice st in 5th st from hook, s c in 1st d c of next d c group, ch 1, sl st in tip of next free petal of same flower, ch 1, sl st in same s c on center, * 1 s c in each of the next 3 d c, picot, 1 s c in each of the next 3 d c, ch 1, sl st in 1st free petal of next flower of same group, ch 1, sl st in same s c on center, ch 5, rice st in 5th st from hook, picot, ch 5, rice st in 5th st from hook, s c in 1st d c of next d c group on center, ch 1, sl st in tip of next free petal of same flower, ch 1, sl st in same s c on center, repeat from * once, 1 s c in each of the next 3 d c on center, picot, 1 s c in each of the next 4 d c, ch 5, rice st in 5th st from hook, cluster st in next picot on center, (cluster st: 3 tr c in same space keeping last loop of each tr c on hook, thread over and pull through all loops at one time) picot, ch 5, rice st in 5th st from hook, s c in 1st d c of next d c group, 1 s c in each of the next 3 d c, picot, 1 s c in each of the next 3 d c, repeat from ** until all flowers are Flower Bouquet Doily

This doily may be made with any of the American Thread Company products listed on the next page:

Material	Quantity	Approx. Size of Doily	Size of Needle
"GEM" Crochet Cotton Article 35, Size 30	1 Ball Tinted Lavender and Yellow 1 Ball Shaded Lavenders 1 Ball Shaded Yellows 1 Ball White 1 Ball Blue 1 Ball Pink 1 Ball Green 1 Ball Yellow	9 inches	Steel 12
or			
"PURITAN" Crochet Cotton Article 40	1 Ball Tinted Lavender and Yellow 1 Ball Shaded Lavenders 1 Ball Shaded Yellows 1 Ball White 1 Ball Blue 1 Ball Pink 1 Ball Green 1 Ball Yellow	11 "	" 7
or			
"DE LUXE" Crochet Cotton Article 346	Same Colors as in "GEM" Crochet Cotton	11 "	" 7
or			
"STAR" Crochet Cotton Article 30, Size 30	"	9 "	" 12
or			
"STAR" Tatting Cotton Article 25	2 Balls Tinted Lavender and Yellow 2 Balls Shaded Lavenders 2 Balls Shaded Yellows 2 Balls White 2 Balls Blue 2 Balls Pink 2 Balls Green 2 Balls Yellow	7 "	" 13

DAISY: With Yellow ch 5, join to form a ring, ch 3 and work 17 d c in ring, join, break thread.

PETAL: With White ch 14, insert hook in any d c, pull loop through, ch 1, 1 s c in next st of ch, 1 s d c in each of the next 3 sts (s d c: thread over hook, insert in st, pull loop through, thread over and work off all loops at one time), 1 d c in each of the next 9 sts, 6 s d c in end st, working on opposite side of ch, 1 d c in each of the next 9 sts, 1 s d c in each of the next 3 sts, 1 s c in next st, sl st in same d c, break thread. Skip 1 d c, work another petal in the next d c. Continue working in the same manner all around. Work a 2nd daisy same as the 1st daisy, joining it to the 1st daisy as illustrated.

FORGET-ME-NOT: With Yellow ch 2, 8 s c in 2nd st from hook, join, break thread. Attach Color, * ch 4, 3 tr c in same space, ch 4, sl st in same space, skip 1 s c, sl st in next s c, repeat from * 3 times, break thread. Work all remaining forget-me-nots in the same manner, always joining in the center tr c of petals.

PANSY: All pansies are worked in same manner, ch 7, join to form a ring, ch 3 (counts as 1 d c), 2 d c in ring, * ch 7, 3 d c in ring, repeat from * 3 times, ch 7, join.

2nd Row—Sl st to loop, ch 3, 12 d c in loop, * 1 s c in center d c of next d c group, 13 d c in next loop, repeat from * once, * s c in center d c of next d c group, ch 4 and work 8 d tr c, 2 tr c, 2 d c with ch 1 between each st in next loop, s c in center d c of next d c group, 2 d c, 2 tr c, 8 d tr c with ch 1 between each st in next loop, ch 4, s c in center d c of next d c group, join, break thread.

LEAF: All leaves are worked with Green in the same manner. Ch 25, s c in 2nd st from hook, 1 s c in next st of ch, 1 s d c in each of the next 2 sts, 1 d c in each of the next 3 sts, 1 tr c in each of the next 8 sts, 1 tr c, 1 d c in next st, 1 d c in each of the next 4 sts, 1 s d c in each of the next 2 sts, 1 s c in each of the next 2 sts, break thread.

Starting with the large group of Blue forget-me-nots, work 6 forget-me-nots, join as illustrated, joining 3, to petals of daisies. Work 2 Pink forget-me-nots, join to Blue forget-me-nots as illustrated. Work a Shaded Lavender pansy, join to Blue forget-me-not. Work a Tinted Lavender and Yellow pansy, join to Pink and 1 Blue forget-me-not. Work a Lavender pansy, join to Pink forget-me-not. Work a Lavender pansy, join to pansy just made, same Pink forget-me-not and daisy. Work a Blue forget-me-not, join to 2 Lavender pansies. Work a group of 3 Pink forget-me-nots, join to Lavender pansy and daisy. Work a

Blue forget-me-not, join to the group of Pink forget-me-nots. Work a Lavender pansy, join to Blue forget-me-not just made and daisy. Work a Yellow pansy, join to Lavender pansy just made and daisy. Work 3 Blue forget-me-nots, joining as illustrated and join to the Yellow pansy and daisy. Work 1 Blue forget-me-not, join to the Yellow pansy. Work a Lavender pansy, join to forget-me-not just made and to 2 Blue forget-me-nots. Work 3 Pink forget-me-nots joining as illustrated and join 1 to Lavender pansy. Work a Tinted Lavender and Yellow pansy, join to daisy. Work a Blue forget-me-not, join to pansy just made. Work a Lavender pansy, join to the flower just made and daisy. Work a Yellow pansy, join to pansy just made and daisy. Work a Pink forget-me-not, join to the Lavender pansy and Yellow pansy. Work a Blue forget-me-not, join to the flower just made and Yellow pansy. Work a Lavender pansy, join to flower just made, to Yellow pansy and to Blue forget-me-not of 1st group made.

Work 5 leaves joining to flowers as illustrated.

Edge—Attach White in free petal of Pink forget-me-not to right of Blue forget-me-not, work a ch long enough to reach next Blue forget-me-not, s c in free petal of flower, work a ch long enough to reach to next pansy, s c (if necessary a d c in order to keep edge round) in 1st petal of flower, continue all around until all flowers are worked. Then work a row of ch 5 loops over ch, ending row with ch 1, d c in joining (110 loops in row).

3rd, 4th and 5th Rows: Ch 4, s c in next loop, repeat from beginning all around ending each row with ch 2, d c in d c.

6th Row: * Ch 4, s c in next loop, repeat from * twice, ** ch 5, skip 1 loop, 2 d c with ch 4 between in next loop, ch 5, skip 1 loop, s c in next loop, * ch 4, s c in next loop, repeat from * 5 times, repeat from ** all around in the same manner ending row with ch 2, d c in d c.

7th Row: * Ch 4, s c in next loop, repeat from * twice, ** ch 6, skip 1 loop, 3
cluster sts with ch 3 between each cluster st in ch 4 loop (cluster st: work 3
tr c in loop keeping last loop of each st on hook, thread over and work off all loops at one time), ch 6, skip 1 loop, s c in next loop, * ch 4, s c in next loop, repeat from * 4 times, repeat from ** all around in the same manner ending row with ch 2, d c in d c.

8th Row: * Ch 4, s c in next loop, repeat from * twice, ** ch 6, skip 1 loop, 2 cluster sts with ch 5 between in next loop, ch 5, 2 cluster sts with ch 5 between in next loop, ch 6, skip 1 loop, s c in next loop, * ch 4, s c in next loop, repeat from * 3 times, repeat from ** all around in the same manner ending row with ch 2, d c in d c.

9th Row: * Ch 4, s c in next loop, repeat from * twice, ch 6, skip 1 loop, 2 cluster sts with ch 3 between in next loop, ch 3, 3 cluster sts with ch 3 between each cluster st in next loop, ch 3, 2 clusters sts with ch 3 between in next loop, ch 6, skip 1 loop, s c in next loop, repeat from beginning all around ending row to correspond.

10th Row: Sl st to 2nd st of loop, ** ch 5, rice st in 5th st from hook (rice st: work 2 tr c in st, keeping last loop of each st on hook, thread over and work off all loops at one time), d c in next loop, ch 3, sl st in d c for picot, ch 5, rice st in 5th st from hook, s c in next loop, ch 5, rice st in 5th st from hook, ch 3, sl st in rice st for picot, ch 5, rice st in 5th st from hook, s c in next cluster st, * ch 5, rice st in 5th st from hook, d c in next cluster st, picot, ch 5, rice st in 5th st from hook, s c in next cluster st, repeat from * twice, ch 5, rice st in 5th st from hook, picot, ch 5, rice st in 5th st from hook, skip 1 loop, s c in next loop, repeat from ** all around, join, break thread. Butterfly Doily

These doilies may be made with any of the American Thread
Company products listed on the next page:

Material for each Dolly	Quantity	Approx. Size of Doily	Size of Needle
"GEM" Crochet Cotton Article 35	1 Ball White 1 Ball any Shaded color Shown	9½ inches	Steel 12
or			
"PURITAN" Crochet Cotton Article 40	1 Ball White 1 Ball any Shaded Color Shown	11½ "	" 7
or			
"DE LUXE" Crochet Cotton Article 346	1 Ball White 1 Ball any Shaded Color Shown	11½ "	" 7
or			
"STAR" Tatting Cotton Article 25	2 Balls White 2 Balls any Shaded Color Shown	7½ "	" 13
or			
"STAR" Crochet Cotton Article 20, Size 30	1 Ball White 1 Ball any Shaded Color Shown	9½ "	" 12
or			
"STAR" Crochet Cotton Article 30, Size 30	1 Ball White 2 Balls any Shaded Color Shown	9½ "	" 12
or			
"STAR" Pearl Cotton Article 90, Size 5	2 Balls White 3 Balls any Shaded Color Shown	11½ "	" 7
or			
"SILLATEEN SANSIL" Article 102	1 Ball White 2 Balls any Shaded Color Shown	10½	" 10

BODY: Top of Head—With Shaded color ch 4, sl st in 4th st from hook (feeler), ch 25, s c in 2nd st from hook, 1 s c in each of the next 19 sts of ch, ch 1, turn.

2nd Row—1 s c in 1st s c, sl st in next s c, 1 s c in each of the next 17 s c, sl st in last st, break thread.
LARGE RIGHT WING: Ch 4, 2 d c in 4th st from hook, ch 1, turn.
2nd Row—2 s c in 1st d c, 1 s c in next d c, 2 s c in next st, ch 1, turn.

3rd and 4th Rows—1 s c in each s c, ch 1, turn.
5th Row—1 s c in 1st s c, 1 d c in each of the next 3 s c, 1 s c in next

s c, ch 5 and without turning and working down long side, d c in next row, ch 2, d c in next row, repeat from * twice, ch 2, 1 d c, ch 2, 1 d c in point (lower edge of wing), working up opposite side, * ch 2 d c in next row, repeat from * 4 times, ch 2, d c in same space, * ch 2, tr c in next d c, repeat from * twice, ch
2, d c in the same space with 1st ch 5, ch 2, join in 3rd st of ch.

Next Row—Sl st into loop, * ch 4, sl st in next loop, repeat from * all around, break thread.
SMALL RIGHT WING: Ch 4, 2 d c in 4th st from hook, ch 1, turn.
2nd Row—1 s c in 1st d c, 2 s c in next d c, 1 s c in next st, ch 1, turn.
3rd Row—1 s c in each s c, ch 1, turn.
4th Row—1 s c in 1st s c, 1 d c in each of the next 2 s c, 1 s c in next s c, (top of wing), do not turn.

5th Row—Working down long side, ch 5, 1 d c in next row, * ch 2, d c in next row, repeat from * once, ch 2, 1 d c, ch 2, 1 d c in point, working up opposite side, * ch 2, d c in next row, repeat from * 3 times, ch 2, d c in the same space, ch 2, tr c in next d c, ch 2, tr c in next d c, ch 2, d c in the same space with ch 5, ch 2, join in 3rd st of ch.

Next Row—Start to join wings. Sl st into loop, ch 2, sl st in 3rd loop to right of center from lower edge of large wing, ch 2, sl st in next loop of small wing, * ch 2, sl st in next loop towards lower edge of large wing, ch 2, sl st in next loop of small wing, repeat from * once, * ch 4, sl st in next loop of small wing, repeat from * around the remainder of the small wing, break thread. Work 2 left wings in the same manner as right wing to the joining.

For joining work 4 loops on the small wing, then join the next 3 loops to corresponding loops on the left side of the large wing and finish the same as other small wing.
To join wings to body, ch 4, sl st in 4th st from hook for other feeler,

ch 4, sl st in 1st s c of 2nd row of body (top of head), 1 sl st in each of the next 2 sts, ch 2, sl st in 3rd free loop to right of joining of large left wing, ch 2, skip 1 st on body, sl st in next st, ch 2, sl st in next free loop of same wing, ch 2, skip 1 s c of body, sl st in next s c, ch 2, sl st in next free loop of same wing, ch 2, skip 2 s c of body, sl st in next st, ch 2, sl st in 1st free loop of small wing, ch 2, skip 2 s c of body, sl st in next s c, * ch 2, sl st in next loop of small wing, ch 2, skip 1 s c of body, sl st in next st, repeat from * once, sl st down the remainder of body to point, work 3 s c in point then sl st in each of the next 3 sts up opposite side, ch 2, sl st in 3rd loop of small right wing to right of joining and join the 2 left wings same as opposite 2 wings, break thread.

Work 6 more butterflies in the same manner.

IF YOU ARE MAKING SMALL CENTER (3½ INCHES) SHOWN on page 33: With White ch 8, join to form a ring, ch 3, 13 d c in ring, join in 3rd st of ch.

2nd Row—* Ch 4, s c in next d c, repeat from * all around ending row with ch 1, d c in same space as beginning (this brings thread in position for next row).

3rd Row—* Ch 4, s c in next loop, repeat from * all around, ending row with ch 1, d c in d c (14 loops).

4th Row—Ch 3, 2 d c in same space keeping last loop of each d c on hook, thread over and pull through all loops at one time, * ch 5, cluster st in next loop (cluster st: 3 d c in next loop keeping last loop of each d c on hook, thread over and pull through all loops at one time), repeat from * all around, ch 5, join to 1st cluster st.

5th Row—Ch 3, 4 d c in same space, 5 d c in next cluster st, repeat from * all around, join.

6th Row—Ch 3, 1 d c in each of the next 4 d c, * ch 2, 1 d c in each of the next 5 d c, repeat from * all around, ch 2, join.

7th Row—Ch 3, 1 d c in each of the next 4 d c, * ch 2, d c in next loop, ch 2, 1 d c in each of the next 5 d c, repeat from * all around ending row with ch 2, d c in next loop, ch 2, join.

8th Row—Ch 3, 1 d c in each of the next 4 d c, * ch 3, s c in next d c, ch 3, 1 d c in each of the next 5 d c, repeat from * all around ending row with ch 3, s c in next d c, ch 3, join.

9th Row—Ch 3, 1 d c in each of the next 4 d c keeping last loop of each d c on hook, thread over and pull through all loops at one time, * ch 4, 1 d c, ch
3, 1 d c in next s c, ch 4, 5 d c cluster st over next 5 d c, repeat from * all around, ending row to correspond.

10th Row—* Ch 5, skip 1 loop, 2 d c, ch 3, 2 d c in next loop, ch 5, s c in next 5 d c cluster st, repeat from * all around.
11th Row—* Ch 6, skip 1 loop, 2 d c, ch 3, 2 d c (shell) in next loop, ch 6, s c in next s c, repeat from * all around.

12th Row—Sl st to center of shell, ch 3, d c in same space, ch 1, sl st in 2nd free loop from body of lower right wing of any butterfly, * ch 1, 2 d c in same space of center, ch 3, s c in next loop, ch 3, sl st in lower edge of body of same butterfly, ch 3, s c in next loop of center, ch 3, 2 d c in center of next shell, ch 1, sl st in 2nd free loop from body of lower left wing of same butterfly, ch 1, 2 d c in same space on center, ch 3, s c in next loop of center, ch 3, cluster st in next s c of center, ch 3, skip 1 loop of same wing of butterfly, sl st in next loop, ch 3, sl st in 4th free loop from body of lower right wing of next butterfly, ch 3, sl st in top of cluster st just made on center, ch 3, s c in next loop of center, ch 3, 2 d c in center of next shell, ch 1, skip 1 loop of butterfly, sl st in next loop of same wing (2nd loop from body), repeat from * until all butterflies are joined, completing the joining of the 1st butterfly.

Joining Motif between Butterflies—With White ch 6, join to form a ring, ch 1, s c in ring, d tr c (3 times over hook) in 3rd free loop of top wing on right hand side of butterfly, s c in ring, skip 1 loop of same wing, d tr c in next loop, s c in ring, d tr c in 1st free loop of lower wing of same butterfly, s c in ring, working up opposite side of next butterfly, d tr c in 1st free loop of lower wing next to the joining of wings, s c in ring, d tr c in 1st free loop of top wing, s c in ring, skip 1 loop, d tr c in next loop of same wing, s c in ring, join, break thread.

IF YOU ARE MAKING BASIC DOILY No. 1 SHOWN ON Page 4 - Work 12 butterflies as above.

Attach White in any loop and work 2 s c, ch 3, 2 s c in same loop, * ch 1, s c in 2nd loop from body of lower right hand wing of butterfly, ch 1, 2 s c, ch 3, 2 s c in same loop of center, 2 s c, ch 3, 2 s c in next loop on center, ch 1, s c in end of body of same butterfly, ch 1, 2 s c, ch 3, 2 s c in same loop on center, 2 s c, ch 3, 2 s c in next loop on center, ch 1, s c in 2nd free loop from body of lower left wing of same butterfly, ch 1, 2 s c, ch 3, 2 s c in same loop on center, 2 s c in next loop on center, ch 1, skip 1 loop of same wing of butterfly, s c in next loop, ch 1, 2 s c, ch 3, 2 s c in same loop on center, ch 1, s c in 4th free loop of lower right wing of next butterfly, ch 1, 2 s c in same loop on center, 2 s c, ch 3, 2 s c in next loop on center, repeat from * until all butterflies are joined, break thread.

IF YOU ARE MAKING BASIC DOILY No. 2 SHOWN ON Page 6 - Work 10 butterflies.

Attach White in 1st d c of any d c group, s c in same space, * 1 d c in each of the next 3 d c, ch 1, sl st in 2nd free loop from body of lower right ring, ch 1, sl st in top of d c just made on center to complete picot, 1 d c in each of the next 2 d c on center, s c in next d c, ch 5, cluster st in next picot, ch 1, sl st in end of body, ch 1, sl st in top of cluster st, ch 5, 1 s c in next d c, 1 d c in each of the next 3 d c, ch 1, sl st in 2nd free loop from body of lower left wing, ch 1, complete picot, 1 d c in each of the next 2 d c, s c in next d c, ch 5, cluster st in next picot on center, ch 3, skip 1 loop of same wing of butterfly, sl st in next loop, ch 5, 2 d c in 4th st from hook leaving last loop of each d c on hook, thread over and pull through all loops at one time, ch 1, sl st in 4th free loop from body of lower right wing of next butterfly, ch 3, sl st in top of cluster st on center, ch 5, 1 s c in next d c, repeat from * all around until all butterflies are joined, break thread.

Work the joining motifs between butterflies same as on Small Center. Cameo Girl Doily

This doily may be made with any of the American Thread Company products listed on the next page:

Material	Quantity	Approx. Size of Doily	Size of Needle
"GEM" Crochet Cotton Article 35, Size 30	1 Ball Cream 1 Ball Iridescent 1 Ball Pink 1 Ball Fuchsia 1 Ball Tinted Pink and Yellow 1 Ball White	5 inches	Steel 12
or			
"STAR" Tatting Cotton Article 25	1 Ball Iridescent 1 Ball Pink 1 Ball Fuchsia 1 Ball Tinted Pink and Yellow 2 Balls White	7 "	" 13
or			
"DE LUXE" Crochet Cotton Article 346	1 Ball Cream 1 Ball Iridescent 1 Ball Pink 1 Ball Rose 1 Ball Tinted Pink and Yellow 1 Ball White	11 "	" 7

With Cream ch 4, s c in 2nd st from hook, 1 s c in each st of ch, ch 1, turn.

2nd and 3rd Rows—1 s c in each s c, ch 1 to turn each row.

4th and 5th Rows—Working in s c increase 1 s c at the beginning and end of each row.

6th Row—Increase 2 s c at the beginning and end of row. Work 1 row even, break thread.

8th Row—Attach Fuchsia (substitute Rose for Fuchsia if "De Luxe" Crochet Cotton is used) and work 1 s c in each s c, break thread, do not turn.

9th Row—Attach Tinted Pink and Yellow, ch 3, 1 d c, ch 3, 2 d c in same space, skip 1 s c, 2 d c, ch 3, 2 d c (shell) in next s c, * skip 2 s c, shell in next s c, repeat from * once, skip 1 s c, shell in next s c, break thread, do not turn. 10th Row—Attach Fuchsia, s c in same space, 1 s c in next d c, * 3 s c in next loop, 1 s c in each of the next 4 d c, repeat from * 3 times, 3 s c in the next loop, 1 s c in each of the next 2 d c, break thread, do not turn.

11th Row—Skip 8 s c, attach Fuchsia in next s c, working in back loop of st, s c in same space, * skip 3 s c, 1 s c in each of the next 4 s c, repeat from * once, skip 3 s c, 1 s c in next s c. Work 1 row even in s c working in both loops.

13th Row—Decrease 1 s c at the beginning and end of row (to decrease: insert hook in st, pull loop through, insert in next st, pull through thread over and work off all loops at one time). Work 1 row even. Repeat the last 2 rows once, then work one more row even, break thread. Do not turn work.

18th Row—Attach Pink, ch 5, s c in same space, * ch 5, s c in next s c, repeat from * 4 times, ch 5, s c in the same space (7 loops), ch 7, turn.
19th Row—S c in next loop, * ch 5, s c in next loop, repeat from * 5 times, ch 3, d c in 2nd st from end of last loop, ch 7, turn (8 loops). Continue working the same as the last row, always having 1 more loop in each row until there are 13 loops.
25th Row—S c over ch 3, * ch 5, s c in next loop, repeat from * across the row, turn.
26th Row—Ch 9, s c in next loop, * ch 6, s c in next loop, repeat from * across the row, turn.
Repeat the last row twice.

29th Row—Ch 10, s c in next loop, * ch 7, s c in next loop, repeat from * across the row, turn.
Repeat 29th row 3 times, ending last row with ch 6, tr c in the last loop, ch 5, turn.

33rd Row—S c over ch 6, * ch 7, s c in next loop, repeat from * twice, ch 3, s c in same loop, repeat from 1st * twice, * ch 7, s c in next loop, repeat from * twice, ch 5, s c in the same space, break thread. Work 3 more dresses in the same manner.

Right Sleeve—With right side of work toward you, attach Tinted Pink and Yellow in 7th s c from end of 10th row, working in back loop of st, * ch 3, s c in next s c, repeat from * twice, * ch 5, s c in next s c, repeat from * once, ch 7, turn.

2nd Row—S c in next loop, ch 5, s c in next loop, * ch 3, s c in next loop, repeat from * twice, turn.
3rd Row—* Ch 3, s c in next loop, repeat from * twice, * ch 5, s c in next loop, repeat from * once, ch 5, turn.
4th Row—Same as 2nd row.
5th Row—* Ch 3, s c in next loop, repeat from * twice, ch 1, turn.
6th Row—* S c in next loop, repeat from * twice, break the thread. Work 3 more right sleeves in the same manner.

Left Sleeve—With the wrong side of work toward you and working in front loop of st, work sleeve in same manner to 3rd row ending last row with ch 3.

4th Row—Join to 4th st of corresponding loop of right sleeve of 1st dress, ch
1, s c in next loop of sleeve of 2nd dress, complete sleeve same as right sleeve. Continue working sleeves on remaining dresses, joining in the same manner.
With the right side of work toward you, attach Fuchsia in 1st s c of sleeve, s c in the same space, 1 s c in each of the next 2 s c, break thread.

Right Arm—With the right side of work toward you, attach Cream in 1st s c of sleeve edge, working in back loop of st, s c in same space, 1 s c in each of the next 2 s c, ch 1 to turn all rows.

Next Row—Working in both loops, 1 s c in each s c.
3rd Row—2 s c in 1st s c, skip 1 s c, sl st in next st.
4th Row—Sl st in sl st, skip 1 s c, 2 s c in next s c.
Repeat the last 2 rows once, then repeat the 3rd row. Work 1 row even.
9th Row—Decrease in 1st 2 sts, s c in next s c. Work 2 rows even, break thread.

Left Arm—With the wrong side of work toward you, attach Cream in 1st s c of left sleeve, working 1st row in front loop of st, then work same as right arm. Sew 2 inner sts of the last row of arms together.

Joining Motif—With the wrong side of work toward you and arms facing upward, attach White in 1st s c of 1st arm, ch 9, s c in last s c of 2nd arm, ch 5, turn.

2nd Row—S c in loop, ch 6, s c in same space, ch 7, s c in same space, ch 6, s c in same space, ch 2, d c in same space with starting ch, ch 3, turn.

3rd Row—2 d c over ch 2, ch 5, 3 d c in next loop, ch 7, 3 tr c in next loop, ch
7, 3 tr c in same space, ch 7, 3 d c in next loop, ch 5, 3 d c in next loop, ch 3, turn.

4th Row—1 d c in each of the next 2 d c keeping last loop of each st on hook, thread over and work off all loops at one time, ch 5, sl st in top of st just made for picot, ch 5, s c in next loop, ch 5, 1 d c in each of the next 3 d c keeping last loop of each st on hook, thread over and work off all loops at one time (d c cluster st), ch 7, s c in next loop, ch 7, 1 tr c cluster st over next 3 tr c, ch 7, 1-3 tr c cluster st over next loop, ch 7, 1 tr c cluster st over next 3 tr c, ch 7, s c in next loop, ch 7, d c cluster st over next 3 d c, ch 5, s c in next loop, ch 5, d c cluster st over next 3 d c, ch 5, turn.

5th Row—Sl st in top of st just made, ch 5, s c in next loop, repeat from * once, ch 6, s c in next loop, ch 7, s c in next loop, ch 11, s c in next loop, ch 13, s c in next loop, ch 11, s c in next loop, ch 7, s c in next loop, ch 6, s c in next loop, ch 5, s c in next loop, ch 2, d c in cluster st, turn.

6th Row—Ch 3, join to 4th st from beginning of 4th large loop from lower edge on side of skirt, ch 3, s c in next loop of motif, ch 3, s c in 4th st of next loop of skirt, ch 3, s c in next loop of motif, ch 3, s c in 4th st of next loop of skirt, ch 4, s c in next loop of motif, ch 7, skip 1 loop of skirt, s c in 1st st of small loop of skirt, ch 11, s c in next loop of motif, ch 9, s c in next loop, ch 9, s c in next loop, ch 11, join to 1st st of small loop of next skirt, ch 7, s c in next loop of motif, ch 4, skip 1 loop of skirt, s c in 4th st from end of next loop of skirt, ch 3, s c in next loop of motif, * ch 3, s c in 4th st of next loop of skirt, ch 3, s c in next loop of motif, repeat from * once, break thread.

EDGE—Attach White in 1st small loop of skirt, 3 s c in same space, * 7 s c in each of the next 3 loops, 3 s c in next loop, repeat from * 3 times, * ch 7, s c in next loop, repeat from * 3 times, ch 7, 3 s c in next loop, repeat from 1st * all around, ending row to correspond, join.

2nd Row—Sl st to next s c, ch 3, 1 d c, ch 3, 2 d c in same space, * ch 3, s c in center st of next loop, ch 5, 2 tr c, ch 3, 2 tr c in center st of next loop (tr c shell), ch 5, s c in center st of next loop, ch 3, d c shell in center st of next loop, repeat from * 3 times, ch 3, s c in next loop, * ch 8, s c in next loop, repeat from * 3 times, ch 3, d c shell in center st of next loop, repeat from 1st * all around, ending row to correspond, join.

3rd Row—* 2 s c, ch 3, 2 s c in next loop, skip 2 d c, 3 s c in next loop, 5 s c in next loop, skip 2 tr c, 2 s c, ch 3, 2 s c in next loop, skip 2 tr c, 5 s c in next loop, 3 s c in next loop, skip 2 d c, repeat from * 3 times, 2 s c, ch 3, 2 s c in next loop, skip 2 d c, 3 s c in next loop, 7 s c in next loop, ch 3, sl st in last s c for picot, 5 s c in next loop, 2 tr c in next s c, ch 3, sl st in last tr c for picot, 1 tr c in same space, 5 s c in next loop, 1 s c in next loop, ch 3, sl st in s c for picot, 6 s c in same loop, 3 s c in next loop, skip 2 d c, repeat from beginning all around ending row to correspond, join, break thread.

Bouquet—With Iridescent, ch 2, 6 s c in 2nd st from hook, join.
2nd Row—* Ch 5, sl st in same space (picot loop), ch 2, sl st in next s c, repeat from * all around.
3rd Row—* Ch 5, sl st in same space, ch 2, sl st in next ch 2 loop, repeat from * all around keeping ch 2 in the back of the picot loop.
4th Row—Work in the same manner as last row having ch 3 between each picot loop, join, break thread.
Work three more bouquets in the same manner. Sew in position as illustrated.
Hat—With Tinted Pink and Yellow, ch 5, join to form a ring, ch 3 and work 12 d c in ring, join.
2nd Row—Ch 1, working in the back loop of st, work 2 s c in each s c, join, break thread.

3rd Row—Attach Fuchsia, s c in same space, 1 s c in each of the next 2 s c, 2 s d c in next s c, 2 s d c in next s c, 1 s d c in next s c, 1 d c in next s c, 2 d c in next s c, 1 d c in next s c, * 1 t r c in next s c, 2 tr c in next s c, repeat from * once, * 2 tr c in next s c, 1 tr c in next s c, repeat from * once, 1 d c in next s c, 2 d c in next s c, 1 d c in next s c, 1 s d c in next sc, 2 s d c in next s c, 2 s d c in next s c, 1 s c in each of the next 3 s c, join, break thread leaving an end long enough to sew to top of head.

Work another hat in the same manner working to the 3rd tr c of the last row, join to corresponding tr c on the side of the hat, complete row. Work 3rd hat joining in the same manner. Work 4th hat, joining hat on both sides.

Sew hats to neck as illustrated. Holly Wreath Doily

These doilies may be made with any of the American Thread
Company products listed on the next page:

Material for each Doily	Quantity	Approx. Size of Doily	Size of Needle
"GEM" Crochet Cotton Article 35, Size 30	1 Ball White 1 Ball Green 1 Ball Red	9 inches	Steel 12
or			
"PURITAN" Crochet Cotton Article 40	1 Ball White 1 Ball Green 1 Ball Red	11 "	" 7
or			
"DE LUXE" Crochet Cotton Article 346	1 Ball White 1 Ball Green 1 Ball Red	11 "	" 7
or			
"STAR" Tatting Cotton Article 25	2 Balls White 2 Balls Green 1 Ball Red	7 "	" 13
or			
"STAR" Crochet Cotton Article 20, Size 30	1 Ball White 1 Ball Green 1 Ball Red	9 "	" 12
or			
"STAR" Crochet Cotton Article 30, Size 30	1 Ball White 2 Balls Green 1 Ball Red	9 "	" 12
or			
"STAR" Pearl Cotton Article 90, Size 5	2 Balls White 2 Balls Green 1 Ball Red	11 "	" 7
or			
"SILLATEEN SANSIL" Article 102	1 Ball White 2 Balls Green 1 Ball Red	10 "	" 10

Leaf: With Green starting at lower edge, ch 3, 2 d c in 3rd st from hook, ch 3, turn.

2nd Row—D c in same space, 1 d c in next d c, 2 d c in next st, ch 3, turn.

3rd Row—2 d c in the same space, 1 d c in each of the next 3 d c, 3 d c in end st, ch 3, turn.
4th Row—1 s c in 2nd st from hook, 1 s c in next st of ch, 1 d c in each of the next 8 d c, 3 d c in next st, ch 1, turn.

5th Row—Sl st in each of the next 2 d c, ch 3, 2 d c in next d c, 1 d c in each of the next 7 d c, 3 d c in next d c, ch 3, turn.
6th Row—2 d c in the same space, 1 d c in each of the next 11 d c, 2 d c in next st, ch 3, turn.
7th Row—1 s c in 2nd st from hook, 1 s c in next st of ch, 1 d c in each of the next 11 d c, 3 d c in next d c, ch 3, turn.
8th Row—Same as 6th row.
9th Row—2 d c in the same space, 1 d c in each of the next 11 d c, 3 d c in next d c, ch 3, turn.
10th row—1 s c in 2nd st from hook, 1 s c in next st of ch, 1 d c in each of the next 17 sts, ch 1, turn.
11th Row—1 sl st in each of the next 3 d c, ch 3, 1 d c in each of the next 13 d c, ch 3, turn.
12th Row—Same as 9th row.
13th Row—1 s c in 2nd st from hook, 1 s c in next st of ch, 1 d c in each of next 14 d c, ch 1, turn.
14th Row—Sl st in each of the next 2 d c, ch 3, 1 d c in each of the next 10 d c, ch 1, turn.

15th Row—Sl st in each of the next 3 d c, ch 3, 1 d c in each of the next 6 d c, ch 1, turn.
16th Row—Sl st in each of the next 3 d c, ch 2, 1 d c in each of the next 3 d c keeping the last loop of each d c on hook, thread over and pull through all loops at one time, break thread. Work 11 more leaves in the same manner.

IF YOU ARE MAKING BASIC CENTER No. 1 SHOWN ON Page 4 - Attach White in any s c of last row of center, ch 4, 2 tr c in same space keeping last loop of each tr c on hook, thread over and pull through all loops at one time, ch 3, sl st in top of cluster st for picot, ch 4, s c in next loop, ch 1 and with 5 point side of leaf towards center, sl st in 1st point of leaf from lower edge, ch 1, sl st in same s c on center, * ch 4, tr c cluster st in next s c on center, (tr c cluster st: 3 tr c in same space keeping last loop of each tr c on hook, thread over and pull through all loops at one time), ch 3, sl st in top of cluster st for picot, ch 4, s c in next loop on center, ch 1, sl st in next point of same leaf, ch 1, sl st in same s c on center, repeat from * once, ch 4, tr c cluster st in next s c on center, picot, ch 4, s c in next loop, picot, ch 4, tr c cluster st in next s c, picot, ch 4, s c in next loop, ch 1, sl st in 1st point from lower edge of next leaf, ch 1, sl st in same s c on center, repeat from 1st * until all leaves are joined, break the thread.

BERRY: With Red ch 2, 8 s c in 2nd st from hook, without joining rows, work 2 s c in each s c.
3rd and 4th Rows—1 s c in each s c.

5th Row—1 s c in next s c, decrease in next 2 sts (to decrease: * insert hook in next st, pull loop through, repeat from *, thread over and pull through all loops at one time), repeat from beginning all around. Fill with cotton or Red yarn, then decrease every other st until 3 sts remain, draw together, break thread leaving an end. Work 11 more berries in the same manner and sew in position as illustrated.

IF YOU ARE MAKING BASIC CENTER No. 2 SHOWN ON Page 6 - Work 10 leaves same as for basic center No. 1 joining to center as follows: attach White in 1st d c of any d c group, ch 3, 1 d c in each of the next 3 d c, ch 1, join in 1st point from lower edge of leaf always having the 5 point side of leaf next to center, * ch 1, d c in same space on center, 1 d c in each of the next 3 d c, ch 3, s c in next loop, ch 3, sl st in next point of same leaf, ch 3, s c in next loop on center, ch 3, 1 d c in each of the next 4 d c, ch 1, sl st in next point of same leaf, ch 1, d c in same space on center, 1 d c in each of the next 3 d c, ch 3, s c in next loop, ch 7, sl st in 4th st from hook for picot, ch 3, s c in next loop, ch 3, 1 s c in each of the next 4 d c, ch 1, sl st in 1st point from lower edge of next leaf, repeat from * until all leaves are joined, break the thread. Work 20 berries the same as for Basic Center No. 1 and sew in position between leaves as illustrated catching the lower edge of the leaf and next free point of previous leaf when sewing.

Ruffled Doilies

9 Ruffled Doily Patterns Edited and printed by:

CraftBindings.com

* (Asterisk)—This sign indicates that the instructions immediately following are to be repeated the given number of times plus the original.
** Are used in the same way.
Abbreviations

St - stitch
sl st - slip stitch
Ch - chain
Lp - loop
Hk - hook
Sc - single crochet Dc - double crochet Hdc - half double crochet Trc - treble crochet Dtrc - double treble crochet Yo - yarn over
Tog - together
Inc - increase
Dec - decrease

Sk - skip
Blossom Ruffle

Materials Required:
Crochet Cotton, Article 40
4 balls White, Cream or Ecru
Crochet hook No. 7
Approximate size: 17½ inches in diameter without ruffle
Chain (ch) 5, join to form a ring, ch 1 and work 8 single crochet (sc) in ring, join in 1st sc.

2nd Round. Ch 3, double crochet (dc) in same space, * ch 3, 2 dc in next sc keeping last loop of each dc on hook, thread over and work off all loops at one time, repeat from * 6 times, ch 3, join.

3rd Round. Slip stitch (sl st) into loop, ch 4, treble crochet (tr c) in same space, ch 2, 2 tr c in same space, * ch 2, 2 tr c, ch 2, 2 tr c in next loop, repeat from * all around, ch 2, join in 4th st of ch.

4th Round. Ch 4, tr c in same space, * tr c in next tr c, ch 2, tr c in next tr c,
2 tr c in next tr c, ch 5, 2 tr c in next tr c, repeat from * all around ending to correspond, ch 5, join.

5th Round. Ch 4, 1 tr c in each of the next 3 tr c, * 1 tr c in each of the next 2 tr c keeping last loop of each tr c on hook, thread over and work off all loops at one time (2 tr c cluster), ch 5, 2 tr c in center st of next loop, ch 5, 2 tr c cluster over next 2 tr c, 1 tr c in each of the next 2 tr c, repeat from * all around ending to correspond, ch 5, join in 1st tr c.

6th Round. Ch 4, 1 tr c in each of the next 3 sts keeping last loop of each tr c on hook, thread over and work off all loops at one time, * ch 5, skip 1 loop, 2 tr c in next tr c, ch 3, 3 tr c in next tr c, ch 3, tr c in next loop, ch 3, 4 tr c cluster over next tr c group, repeat from * all around ending to correspond, ch 3, join in 1st cluster.

7th Round. Sl st to next tr c, ch 4, tr c in next tr c, * ch 3, 2 tr c in next tr c, 1 tr c, ch 2, 1 tr c in next tr c, 2 tr c in next tr c, ch 2, skip 1 loop, tr c in next loop, ch 5, tr c in next loop, ch 2, 1 tr c in each of the next 2 tr c, repeat from * all around ending to correspond, ch 2, join in 4th st of ch.

8th Round. Ch 4, tr c in next tr c, * ch 2, 2 tr c in next tr c, 1 tr c in each of the next 2 tr c, 4 tr c in next loop, 1 tr c in each of the next 2 tr c, 2 tr c in next tr c, ch 4, skip 1 loop, tr c in next loop, ch 4, skip next tr c and next loop, 1 tr c in each of the next 2 tr c, repeat from * all around ending to correspond, ch 4, join in 4th st of ch.

9th Round. Ch 4, tr c in next tr c, ch 3, * 2 tr c in next tr c, 1 tr c in each of the next 5 tr c, 2 tr c in next tr c, 1 tr c in each of the next 4 tr c, 2 tr c in next tr c, ch 3, skip 1 loop, tr c in next loop, ch 3, 1 tr c in each of the next 2 tr c, ch 3, repeat from * all around ending to correspond, join.

10th Round. Ch 4, tr c in same space, * ch 3, 3 tr c in next tr c, ch 4, 5 tr c cluster over next 5 tr c, ch 4, 1 tr c in each of the next 5 tr c, ch 4, 5 tr c cluster over next 5 tr c, ch 4, tr c in next loop, ch 4, skip 1 loop, 2 tr c in next tr c, repeat from * all around ending to correspond, ch 4, join.

11th Round. Ch 4, tr c in next tr c, * ch 3, 2 tr c in next tr c, 1 tr c, ch 2, 1 tr c in next tr c, 2 tr c in next tr c, ch 5, skip 1 loop, tr c in next loop, ch 5, 5 tr c cluster over next 5 tr c, ch 5, tr c in next loop, ch 5, tr c in next loop, ch 5, skip 1 loop, 1 tr c in each of the next 2 tr c, repeat from * all around ending to correspond, ch 5, join.

12th Round. Ch 4, tr c in next tr c, ** ch 3, 2 tr c in next tr c, 1 tr c in each of the next 2 tr c, 4 tr c in next loop, 1 tr c in each of the next 2 tr c, 2 tr c in next tr c, ch 3, tr c in next loop, * ch 5, tr c in next loop, repeat from * twice, ch 5, skip 1 loop, 1 tr c in each of the next 2 tr c, repeat from ** all around ending to correspond, ch 5, join.

13th Round. Ch 4, tr c in next tr c, ** ch 3, 2 tr c in next tr c, 1 tr c in each of the next 4 tr c, 2 tr c in next tr c, 1 tr c in each of the next 5 tr c, 2 tr c in next tr c, ch 3, tr c in next loop, * ch 5, tr c in next loop, repeat from * twice, ch 5, skip 1 loop, 1 tr c in each of the next 2 tr c, repeat from ** all around ending to correspond, ch 5, join.

14th Round. Ch 4, tr c in next tr c, ** ch 5, 5 tr c cluster over next 5 tr c, ch
5, 1 tr c in each of the next 5 tr c, ch 5, 5 tr c cluster over next 5 tr c, ch 3, tr c in next loop, * ch 5, tr c in next loop, repeat from * twice, ch

5, skip 1 loop, 1 tr c in each of the next 2 tr c, repeat from ** all around ending to correspond, ch 5, join.

15th Round. Ch 4, 2 tr c in same space, ** ch 2, 3 tr c in next tr c, ch 3, tr c in next loop, ch 5, tr c in next loop, ch 5, 5 tr c cluster over next 5 tr c, * ch 5, tr c in next loop, repeat from * 4 times, ch 5, skip 1 loop, 3 tr c in next tr c, repeat from ** all around ending to correspond, ch 5, join.

16th Round. Ch 4, tr c in same space, ** 1 tr c in each of the next 2 tr c, 4 tr c in next loop, 1 tr c in each of the next 2 tr c, 2 tr c in next tr c, ch 5, skip 1 loop, tr c in next loop, * ch 5, tr c in next loop, repeat from * 5 times, ch 5, skip 1 loop, 2 tr c in next tr c, repeat from ** all around ending to correspond, ch 5, join.

17th Round. Ch 4, tr c in same space, ** 1 tr c in each of the next 4 tr c, 2 tr c in next tr c, 1 tr c in each of the next 5 tr c, 2 tr c in next tr c, ch 3, tr c in next loop, * ch 5, tr c in next loop, repeat from * 5 times, ch 5, skip 1 loop, 2 tr c in next tr c, repeat from ** all around ending to correspond, ch 5, join.

18th Round. Ch 4, 4 tr c cluster over next 4 tr c, ** ch 5, 1 tr c in each of the next 5 tr c, ch 5, 5 tr c cluster over next 5 tr c, ch 3, tr c in next loop, * ch 5, tr c in next loop, repeat from * 5 times, ch 5, skip 1 loop, 5 tr c cluster over next 5 tr c, repeat from ** all around ending to correspond, ch 5, join.

19th Round. Sl st into loop, ch 9, ** 5 tr c cluster over next 5 tr c, * ch 5, tr c in next loop, repeat from * 9 times, ch 5, repeat from ** all around ending last repeat with ch 2, dc in 4th st of ch (this brings thread in position for next round).

20th Round. Ch 10, tr c in next loop, * ch 6, tr c in next loop, repeat from * all around ending with ch 3, dc in 4th st of ch.

21st Round. Ch 4, tr c in same space, * ch 5, tr c in next loop, repeat from * all around, ch 5, join.

22nd Round. Start ruffle: sl st to next loop, * ch 10, sc in same loop, ch 10, sc in same loop, ch 10, sc in same loop, ch 10, sc in next loop, repeat from * all around ending with ch 5, double treble crochet ([d tr c] 3 times over hook) in same space as beginning.

23rd Round. * Ch 10, sc in next loop, repeat from * all around ending with ch 5, d tr c in d tr c.

Repeat the last round 9 times.

Next Round. ** Ch 5, 5 tr c cluster st in next loop (5 tr c cluster st: 5 tr c in same space keeping last loop of each tr c on hook, thread over and work off all loops at one time), ch 4, sl st in top of cluster st for picot, ch 3, 5 tr c in same loop, ch 1, turn, 1 sc in each of the last 5 tr c just made, ch 3, turn, 1 tr c in each of the next 3 sc keeping last loop of each tr c on hook, thread over and work off all loops at one time, ch 4, sl st in top of tr c cluster just made for picot, ch 4, sl st in last sc, ch 3, 5 tr c cluster st in same loop, ch 4, sl st in top of cluster st just made for picot, ch 5, sc in next loop, * ch 9, sl st in 5th st from hook for picot, ch 5, sc in next loop, repeat from * 8 times, repeat from ** all around, join, cut thread.

Tea Time Ruffle

Materials Required:
Crochet Cotton, Article 40
1 ball each Silver Spangle and Pink Spangle
Approximate size: 10¼ inches in diameter
or
Crochet Cotton, Article 40
1 ball each White and Pink or colors of your choice
Approximate size: 9¼ inches in diameter
Crochet hook No. 6

With Silver Spangle or White chain (ch) 8, join to form a ring, * ch 12, single crochet (sc) in ring, repeat from * 6 times, ch 6, double treble crochet ([d tr c] 3 times over hook) in ring, this brings thread into position for next round.

2nd Round. Ch 3, 2 double crochet (dc) in same loop, * ch 8, 3 dc in next loop, repeat from * 6 times, ch 4, treble crochet (tr c) in 3rd stitch (st) of ch.

3rd Round. Ch 3, 2 dc in same loop, * ch 7, sc in center dc of next dc group, ch 7, 3 dc in next loop, repeat from * 6 times, ch 7, sc in center dc of next dc group, ch 7, join in 3rd st of ch.

4th Round. Ch 5, skip 1 dc, sc in next dc, ch 10, slip stitch (sl st) in 5th st from hook for picot, ch 5, sc in next dc, repeat from beginning all around ending to correspond, join.

5th Round. Sl st to loop, ch 3, 2 dc in same loop, * ch 7, sc in next loop to right of picot, sc in next loop to left of picot, keeping picot in front of work ch 7, 3 dc in next loop, repeat from * all around ending to correspond, join in 3rd st of ch.

6th Round. Ch 3, 2 dc in same space, * ch 7, skip next dc, 3 dc in next dc, ch
7, 1 sc in each of the next 2 SC, ch 7, 3 dc in next dc, repeat from *
all around ending to correspond, join.

7th Round. Ch 3, 1 dc in each of the next 2 dc, * ch 5, sc in next loop, ch 5, sl st in sc for picot, ch 5, 1 dc in each of the next 3 dc, sc in next loop, ch 10, sl st in 5th st from hook for picot, ch 5, sc in next loop, 1 dc in each of the next 3 dc, repeat from * all around ending to correspond, join.

8th Round. Ch 3, 1 dc in each of the next 2 dc, * ch 5, 3 dc, ch 5, 3 dc in picot, ch 5, 1 dc in each of the next 3 dc, sc in next loop, ch 4, 1 dc in 4th st from hook, sc in same loop to right of picot, sc in next loop to left of picot, ch 4, 1 dc in 4th st from hook, sc in same loop, 1 dc in each of the next 3 dc, repeat from * all around ending to correspond, join.

9th Round. Ch 3, 1 dc in each of the next 2 dc, ** ch 3, sc in next loop, ch 5, sl st in sc for picot, ch 3, 2 tr c in next loop, * ch 2, 2 tr c in same loop, repeat from * 3 times, ch 3, sc in next loop, ch 5, sl st in sc for picot, ch 3, 1 dc in each of the next 3 dc, ch 3, skip next sc and next loop, 1 sc in each of the next 2 sc, ch 3, 1 dc in each of the next 3 dc, repeat from ** all around ending to correspond, join.

10th Round. Ch 4, 1 tr c in each of the next 2 dc, ** ch 4, sc in next loop to right of picot, sc in next loop to left of picot, ch 4, ** 2 tr c in next loop, * ch
2, 2 tr c in same loop, repeat from * once, ch 2, repeat from 2nd ** 3 times ending with ch 4 instead of ch 2, sc in next loop to right of picot, sc in next loop to left of picot, ch 4, 1 tr c in each of the next 6 dc, repeat from 1st ** all around ending to correspond, join, cut thread.

11th Round. Attach Pink in joining, ch 4, 6 tr c in same space, ch 3, skip next 2 loops, * 2 tr c in next loop, ch 2, 2 tr c in same loop, ch 2, repeat from * 9 times, 2 tr c, ch 2, 2 tr c in next loop, ch 3, skip next 2 loops, 7 tr c in space between next 2 groups of tr c, complete round to correspond, join in 4th st of ch.

12th Round. Sl st to center tr c, ** ch 2, 1 dc in same space, 1 sc in same space, ch 3, sc in next loop, * ch 3, 2 tr c in next loop, ch 5, sl st in top of tr c for picot, 2 tr c in same loop, ch 3, sc in next loop, repeat from * 10 times, ch 3, sc in center tr c of next tr c group, repeat from ** all around, ending to correspond, join, cut thread
Sunburst Ruffle

Materials Required:
Crochet Cotton, Article 40
2 balls each Silver Spangle, Sunshine Spangle, Chartreuse Spangle
and Green Spangle
Approximate size: 16½ inches in diameter
or
Crochet Cotton, Article 40
1 ball each White, Buttercup, Chartreuse and Forest Green
Approximate size: 15½ inches in diameter
Crochet hook No. 7

With Silver Spangle or White chain (ch) 8, join to form a ring, * ch 5, sc in ring, repeat from * 4 times.

2nd Round. Ch 2, 3 sc in 1st loop, * ch 6, 3 sc in next loop, repeat from * 3 times.

3rd Round. * Ch 6, skip next sc, 1 sc in each of the next 2 sc, 3 sc in next loop, repeat from * 4 times.

4th Round. * Ch 6, skip 1 sc, 1 sc in each sc, 3 sc. in next loop, repeat from *
4 times. Repeat the last round, always skipping the 1st sc of each sc group and working 3 sc in each loop until there are 10 rounds of sc and 21 sc in each solid section.

12th Round. * Ch 6, skip 2 sc, 1 sc in each of the next 18 sc, ch 6, sc in next loop, repeat from * 4 times.

13th Round. * Ch 6, skip 2 sc, 1 sc in each of the next 15 sc, ch 6, sc in next loop, ch 6, sc in next loop, repeat from * 4 times.

14th Round. ** Ch 6, skip 2 sc, 1 sc in each of the next 12 sc, * ch 6, sc in next loop, repeat from * twice, repeat from ** 4 times.

15th Round. ** Ch 6, skip 2 sc, 1 sc in each of the next 9 sc, ch 6, sc in next loop, repeat from * 3 times, repeat from ** 4 times.

16th Round. ** Ch 6, skip 1 sc, 1 sc in each of the next 7 sc, * ch 6, sc in next loop, repeat from * 4 times, repeat from ** 4 times.

17th Round. Ch 4, skip 1 sc, double crochet (dc) in next sc, * ch 2, skip 1 sc, dc in next sc, repeat from * once, ch 4, sc in next loop, * ch 6, sc in next loop, repeat from * 4 times, repeat from beginning 3 times, ch 4, skip 1 sc, dc in next sc, ch 2, skip 1 sc, dc in next sc, ch 2, skip 1 sc, dc in next sc, ch 4, sc in next loop, * ch 6, sc in next loop, repeat from * 3 times. 18th Round. Ch 5, dc in next loop, * ch 3, dc in next loop, repeat from * twice, ch 5, sc in next loop, * ch 6, sc in next loop, repeat from * 3 times, repeat from beginning 4 times, but ending last repeat with ch 2, dc in the center of 1st loop (this brings thread in position for next round).

19th Round. Ch 12, sc in same loop where last dc was worked, * ch 12, sc in next loop, repeat from * all around ending with ch 12, join.
20th Round. Ch 1 and work 17 sc over each loop, join.

21st Round. Ch 1 and working in back loop of sts, * 1 sc in each of the next 7 sc, 3 sc in next sc, 1 sc in each of the next 7 sc, skip 2 sc, repeat from * all around, join. Repeat the last round for remainder of doily working 4 more rounds Silver Spangle or White, 6 rounds Sunshine Spangle or Buttercup, 6 rounds Chartreuse, 6 rounds Green, join, cut thread.
The Large Table Ruffle Chain (ch) 7, join to form a ring, ch 1, 12 single crochet (sc) in ring, join in 1st sc.

Materials Required:
Crochet Cotton, Article 40
11 balls White, Cream or Ecru
Crochet hook No. 7
Approximate size: 32 inches in diameter without ruffle

2nd Round. * Ch 3, sc in next sc, repeat from * all around, ch 3, join (12 loops).

3rd Round. Slip stitch (sl st) into loop, ch 6, treble crochet (tr c) in same space, * ch 3, 2 tr c with ch 2 between in next loop, repeat from * all around, ch 3, join in 4th st of ch.

4th Round. Sl st into loop, * ch 3, sc in next loop, repeat from * all around, ch 3, join.
5th Round. Sl st into loop, * ch 4, sc in next loop, repeat from * all around, ch 4, join.

6th Round. Sl st to 2nd st of next loop, * ch 5, sc in next loop, repeat from * all around ending with ch 2, double crochet (dc) in last sl st (this brings thread in position for next round).

7th Round. * Ch 6, sc in next loop, repeat from * all around ending with ch 2, tr c in dc.

8th Round. Ch 4, tr c over tr c, ch 3, sl st in top of tr c just made for picot, tr c over same tr c already worked over, * ch 4, 2 tr c in next loop, ch 3, sl st in top of last tr c for picot, tr c in same loop, repeat from * all around ending with ch 2, dc in 4th st of ch.

9th Round. * Ch 7, sc in next loop, repeat from * all around ending with ch 3, tr c in dc.

10th Round. Ch 5, tr c over tr c, * ch 7, 1 tr c, ch 1, 1 tr c in next loop, repeat from * all around ending with ch 3, tr c in 4th st of ch.

11th Round. * Ch 4, 1 sc, ch 3, 1 sc (picot) in next ch 1 space, ch 4, sc in next loop, repeat from * all around ending last repeat with sl st in tr c.

12th Round. Ch 3, sc in same space, ch 8, * skip the next picot, 1 sc, ch 3, 1 sc in next sc, ch 8, repeat from * all around ending last repeat with ch 4, tr c in joining.

13th Round. * Ch 6, skip the next picot, sc in beginning of next loop, ch 6, sc at end of same loop, repeat from * all around ending with ch 6, skip the next picot, sc in next loop, ch 3, dc in tr c.

14th, 15th, 16th and 17th Rounds. * Ch 6, sc in next loop, repeat from * all around ending each round with ch 3, dc in dc.

18th Round. * Ch 7, sc in next loop, repeat from * all around ending with ch 3, tr c in dc.

19th and 20th Rounds. * Ch 7, sc in next loop, repeat from * all around ending each round with ch 3, tr c in tr c.

21st Round. Same as 8th round but having 5 chs between each tr c group.

22nd Round. Same as 9th round but having ch 8 in each loop and ending with ch 4, tr c in dc.

23rd Round. Same as 10th round.

24th Round. * Ch 3, 1 sc, ch 3, 1 sc (picot) in next ch 1 space, ch 3, sc in next loop, repeat from * all around ending last repeat with sl st in tr c.

25th Round. Ch 3, sc in same space, ch 7, * skip the next picot, 1 sc, ch 3, 1 sc in next sc, ch 7, repeat from * all around ending last repeat with ch 3, tr c in joining.

26th Round. * Ch 5, skip the next picot, sc in beginning of next loop, ch 5, sc in end of same loop, repeat from * all around ending with ch 5, skip the next picot, sc in next loop, ch 2, dc in tr c.

Next 3 Rounds. * Ch 5, sc in next loop, repeat from * all around ending each round with ch 2, dc in dc.

Next 4 Rounds. * Ch 6, sc in next loop, repeat from * all around ending each round with ch 3, dc in dc.

Next Round. * Ch 7, sc in next loop, repeat from * all around ending with ch 3, tr c in dc.

Next 3 Rounds. * Ch 7, sc in next loop, repeat from * all around ending each round with ch 3, tr c in tr c.

Repeat the 8th, 9th and 10th rounds once.

Repeat the 24th, 25th and 26th rounds once.

Work 4 more rounds of ch 5 loops.

Work 5 rounds of ch 6 loops.

Work 5 rounds of ch 7 loops.

Next Round. Same as 8th round.

Next Round. * Ch 6, sc in next loop, repeat from * all around ending with ch 3, dc in dc.

Next Round. Same as last round but ending with ch 1, tr c in dc.

Repeat the last 3 rounds once. Next Round. Same as the 8th round.

Next Round. Same as 9th round but ending last repeat with sl st in dc.

Next Round. Start Ruffle: sl st into loop, * ch 10, sc in same loop, ch 10, sc in same loop, ch 10, sc in same loop, ch 10, sc in next loop, repeat from * all around, do not join this or following rounds. Place a marker at the beginning of each round.

Next 14 Rounds. * Ch 10, sc in next loop, repeat from * all around, join to the last round, cut the thread.

If Smaller Doily is desired, start ruffle in either the 27th or 44th round and work as many rounds of ch 10 loops for ruffle as desired.

The Flower Ruffle

Materials Required:
Crochet Cotton, Article 40
2 balls Shaded Lavender
1 ball each Kelly Green, White and Shaded Yellows
Approximate size: 14 inches x 20 inches
or
Crochet Cotton, Article 40
2 balls Purples and Silver Spangle

1 ball each Green Spangle and Yellow Spangle
2 balls Silver Spangle or colors of your choice
Approximate size: 15½ inches x 22 inches
Crochet hook No. 7
Flower: With Green chain (ch) 10, join to form a ring, ch 1 and work
20 single crochet (sc) in ring, join in 1st sc.

2nd Row. Ch 4, double crochet (dc) in next sc, * ch 1, dc in next sc,
repeat from * all around, ch 1, join in 3rd stitch (st) of chain, cut
thread.
3rd Row. Attach Shaded Lavenders or Purple and Silver Spangle in
any ch 1 space and work 2 sc in each ch 1 space, join.
Next Row. Start petals: ch 1, sc in the same space, 1 sc in each of
the next 4 sc, ch 1 to turn all rows.
** Next Row. 2 sc in 1st sc, 1 sc in each of the next 3 sc, 2 sc in next
sc, ch 1, turn. Work 5 rows even in sc.

Next Row. Decrease 1 st at beginning and end of row (to decrease, *
insert hook in next st, pull loop through, repeat from * once, thread
over and work off all loops at one time).

Next Row. Decrease 1 st at beginning and end of row.

Next Row. * Insert hook in next st, pull loop through, repeat from *
twice, thread over and work off all loops at one time, ch 1, turn, slip
stitch (sl st) down side of petal, 1 sc in each of the next 5 sc of 2nd
row, ch 1, turn, repeat from ** until 8 petals are completed, join, cut
thread.

Attach Green in tip of petal, * ch 2, working down left hand side of
petal, skip 2 rows, sc in next row, repeat from * twice, ch 2, sl st
between petals, * ch 2, working up right hand side of next petal, skip
2 rows, sc in next row, repeat from * twice, ch 2, sc in tip of same
petal, repeat from 1st * around all petals, join, cut thread. Work
another flower in the same manner joining 2 petals of 1st flower to 2

petals of 2nd flower at tip. Work a 3rd flower in the same manner, joining 2 petals of 3rd flower to 2 petals of 2nd flower at tip leaving 2 petals free between joinings.

Stamens: With Shaded Yellows or Yellow Spangle * ch 13, insert hook in 2nd st from hook, pull loop through, insert hook in each of the next 4 sts of ch pulling a loop through each st, thread over and pull through all 6 loops at one time, 1 sl st in each remaining st of ch, repeat from * 4 times, cut the thread. Pull through the center of the flower and sew firmly on the wrong side. Work a set of stamens for each flower in the same manner.

1st Round. Attach White or Silver Spangle in sc of tip of 3rd free petal from lower edge of joining of end flower, sc in same space, * ch 7, skip 1 loop on side of petal, 1 treble crochet (tr c) in each of the next 2 loops keeping last loop of each tr c on hook, skip last loop of same petal and 1st loop of next petal, 1 tr c in each of the next 2 loops keeping last loop of each tr c on hook, thread over and work off all loops at one time (4 tr c cluster), ch 7, sc in sc at tip of same petal, repeat from * twice, ch 7, work a 4 tr c cluster between petal already worked in and next petal, ch 5, 1 tr c in next loop of same petal keeping last loop of st on hook, tr c in 1st loop of next petal of next flower keeping last loop of each tr c on hook, thread over and work off all loops at one time (a 2 tr c cluster at joining), ch 5, 4 tr c cluster between petal already worked in and next petal, ch 7, sc in sc at tip of same petal, ch 7, 4 tr c cluster between petal just worked in and next petal, ch 7, sc in sc at tip of same petal, ch 7, 4 tr c cluster between petal just worked in and next petal, ch 5, 2 tr c cluster at joining same as before, ch 5, 4 tr c cluster between petal just worked in and next petal, * ch 7, sc in sc at tip of same petal, ch 7, 4 tr c cluster between petal just worked in and next petal, repeat from * 5 times, finish opposite side to correspond, ch 7, join.

2nd Round. Ch 9, * 1 dc, ch 3, 1 dc in next 4 tr c cluster, ch 6, dc in next sc at tip of next petal, ch 6, repeat from * twice, 1 dc, ch 3, 1 dc in next 4 tr c cluster, ch 2, 1 tr c, ch 3, 1 tr c in next 2 tr c cluster, ch 2, 1 dc, ch 3, 1 dc in next 4 tr c cluster, * ch 6, dc in next sc at tip of next petal, ch 6, 1 dc, ch 3, 1 dc in next 4 tr c cluster, repeat from * once, ch 2, 1 tr c, ch 3, 1 tr c in next 2 tr c cluster, ch 2, 1 dc, ch 3, 1 dc in next 4 tr c cluster, * ch 6, dc in next sc at tip of next petal, ch 6, 1 dc, ch 3, 1 dc in next 4 tr c cluster, repeat from * 5 times, finish the other side to correspond, ch 6, join in 3rd st of ch. 3rd Round. Ch 6, dc in same space, * ch 6, skip 1 loop, 1 dc, ch 3, 1 dc in next ch 3 loop, ch 6, skip 1 loop, 1 dc, ch 3, 1 dc in next dc, repeat from * twice, ch 6, skip 1 loop, dc in next ch 3 loop, skip next ch 2 loop, 2 double treble crochet ([d tr c] 3 times over hook) in next loop, ch 3, 2 d tr c in same loop, skip next ch 2 loop, dc in next ch 3 loop, ch 6, skip 1 loop, 1 dc, ch 3, 1 dc in next dc, ch 6, skip 1 loop, 1 dc, ch 3, 1 dc in next ch 3 loop, ch 6, skip 1 loop, 1 dc, ch 3, 1 dc in next dc, ch 6, skip 1 loop, dc in next ch 3 loop, skip the next ch 2 loop, 2 d tr c, ch 3, 2 d tr c in next loop, skip next ch 2 loop, dc in next loop, * ch 6, skip 1 loop, 1 dc, ch 3, 1 dc in next dc, ch 6, skip 1 loop, 1 dc, ch 3, 1 dc in next ch 3 loop, repeat from * 5 times, finish opposite side and end to correspond, ch 6, join in 3rd st of ch.

4th Round. Sl st into loop, ch 3, 1 dc, ch 3, 2 dc in same space, * ch 6, skip next ch 6 loop, 2 dc, ch 3, 2 dc (shell) in next ch 3 loop, repeat from * 5 times, ch 6, skip next ch 6 loop, 2 tr c, ch 3, 2 tr c in next ch 3 loop, * ch 6, skip next ch 6 loop, shell in next ch 3 loop, repeat from * twice, ch 6, skip 1 loop, 2 tr c, ch 3, 2 tr c in next ch 3 loop, * ch 6, skip next loop, shell in next ch 3 loop, repeat from * 10 times, finish opposite side and end to correspond, ch 6, join.

5th Round. Sl st into loop, ch 3, 1 dc, ch 3, 2 dc in same space, * ch 7, shell in next shell, repeat from * 6 times, * ch 6, shell in next shell, repeat from * 3 times, * ch 7, shell in next shell, repeat from * 11 times, finish opposite side and end to correspond, ch 7, join.

6th Round. Sl st into shell, ch 3, 1 dc, ch 3, 2 dc in same space, * ch 3, dc in next loop, ch 3, shell in next shell, repeat from * 6 times, * ch 2, dc in next loop, ch 2, shell in next shell, repeat from * 3 times, * ch 3, dc in next loop, ch 3, shell in next shell, repeat from * 11 times, finish opposite side and end to correspond, ch 3, join.

7th Round. Sl st into shell, ch 3, 1 dc, ch 3, 2 dc in same space, * ch 2, skip 1 loop, 1 dc, ch 3, 1 dc in next dc, ch 2, shell in next shell, repeat from * all around ending to correspond, ch 2, join.
8th Round. Sl st into shell, ch 3, 1 dc, ch 3, 2 dc in same space, * ch 2, skip next ch 2 loop, 1 dc, ch 3, 1 dc in next loop, ch 2, shell in next shell, repeat from * all around ending to correspond, ch 2, join.

9th Round. Sl st into shell, * ch 8, skip next ch 2 loop, sc in next ch 3 loop, ch 8, sc in center of next shell, repeat from * all around ending to correspond, join, cut thread.

10th Round. Attach Shaded Lavender or Purple and Silver Spangle in any loop, ch 3, 4 dc in same loop, ch 4, 5 dc in same loop, * ch 1, 5 dc, ch 1, 5 dc in next loop, repeat from * all around, ch 1, join.

11th Round. Ch 4, skip 1 dc, sc in next dc, ch 4, skip 1 dc, dc in next dc, 2 dc in next loop, ch 4, 2 dc in same loop, dc in next dc, * ch 4, skip 1 dc, sc in next dc, repeat from * once, ch 4, skip the ch 1 space, sc in next dc, repeat from beginning all around ending to correspond, join.

12th Round. Sl st into loop, ch 5, sc in next loop, ** ch 5, skip 2 dc, dc in next dc, 2 dc, ch 4, 2 dc in next loop, dc in next dc, * ch 5, sc in next loop, repeat from * 4 times, repeat from ** all around ending to correspond, join, cut thread.

13th Round. Attach Green in ch 4 loop of any point, ch 5, sc in same space, * ch 4, sc in next loop, repeat from * 5 times, ch 4, 1 sc, ch 5,

1 sc in next loop at point, repeat from 1st * all around ending to correspond, join, cut Green.

14th Round. Attach White or Silver Spangle in any ch 5 loop at point, ch 5, dc in same space, * ch 5, 1 dc, ch 2, 1 dc in ch 5 loop at top of next point, repeat from * all around, ch 5, join in 3rd st of ch.

15th Round. Sl st into loop, ch 3, 1 dc, ch 2, 2 dc in same space, * ch 2, sc in center st of next loop, ch 2, 2 dc, ch 2, 2 dc (shell) in next loop, repeat from * all around ending to correspond, join, cut thread. 16th Round. Attach Shaded Yellows or Yellow Spangle in center of any shell, ch 3, dc in same space, * ch 1, sl st in 3rd st from hook for picot, ch 1, 2 dc in same space, ch 3, sc in next sc, ch 3, 2 dc in center of next shell, repeat from * all around ending to correspond, join, cut thread. The Sea Shell Ruffle

Doilies make wonderful gifts. The Sea Shell can be made in 3 hours.

Materials Required:
Crochet Cotton, Article 40
1 ball each Silver Spangle and Aqua Spangle

Approx. Size: 9½ in. diameter with ruffle
or
Crochet Cotton, Article 40
1 ball each White and Turquoise or colors of your choice
Approximate size: 8½ inches in diameter including ruffle. Crochet hook No. 7
With Silver or White chain (ch) 4, join to form a ring, ch 3 and work 11 double crochet (dc) in ring, join in 3rd stitch (st) of ch.

2nd Round. Ch 3, dc in same space, * ch 2, 2 dc in next dc, repeat from * 10 times, ch 2, join in 3rd st of ch.

3rd Round. Slip stitch (sl st) into loop, ch 3, dc in same loop, * ch 2, 2 dc in same loop, 2 dc in next loop, repeat from * 10 times, ch 2, 2 dc in the same loop, join in 3rd st of ch, cut the thread.

4th Round. Attach Aqua Spangle or Turquoise in any ch 2 loop, ch 3, dc in same loop, ch 2, 2 dc in same loop, * ch 2, 2 dc in next ch 2 loop, ch 2, 2 dc in same loop (2 dc shell), repeat from * all around ending with ch 2, join in 3rd st of ch.

5th Round. Sl st into loop of shell, ch 3, dc in same space, ch 2, 2 dc in same space, * ch 3, shell in next shell, repeat from * all around ending with ch 3, join.

6th Round. Sl st into loop of shell, ch 3, dc in same space, ch 3, 2 dc in same space, * ch 4, 2 dc, ch 3, 2 dc in next shell, repeat from * all around ending with ch 4, join.

7th Round. Sl st into loop of shell, ch 3, 2 dc in same space, ch 3, 3 dc in same space, * ch 5, 3 dc, ch 3, 3 dc (3 dc shell) in next shell, repeat from * all around ending with ch 5, join.

8th Round. Sl st into loop of shell, ch 3, 2 dc in same space, ch 3, 3 dc in same space, * ch 6, 3 dc, ch 3, 3 dc in next shell, repeat from *

all around, ch
6, join.

9th Round. Sl st into loop of shell, ch 3, 2 dc in same space, ch 4, 3
dc in same space, * ch 7, 3 dc, ch 4, 3 dc in next shell, repeat from *
all around, ch
7, join.
10th Round. Sl st into loop of shell, ch 4, 3 treble crochet (tr c) in
same space, ch 6, 4 tr c in same space, * ch 7, 4 tr c in next shell, ch
6, 4 tr c in same space, repeat from * all around, ch 7, join, cut
thread.

11th Round. Attach Silver or White in 1st st of ch 6 of any shell, ch 6,
double treble crochet ([d tr c] 3 times over hook) in same loop, * ch 1,
d tr c in same loop, repeat from * 14 times, * ch 1, sc in next loop, ch
1, 16 d tr c with ch 1 between each d tr c in next shell, repeat from *
all around ending with ch 1, sc in next loop, ch 1, join in 5th st of ch,
cut thread.

12th Round. Attach Aqua Spangle or Turquoise in first ch 1 space at
base of scallop, ch 5, d tr c in same space, * 2 d tr c in next ch 1
space, repeat from * all around, join, cut thread.

13th Round. Attach Silver or White in any space between d tr c, sc in
same space, * ch 3, sc in top of sc for picot, ch 1, skip next space, sc
in next space, repeat from * all around, join, cut thread.
The Yellow Bud Ruffle

Materials Required:
Crochet Cotton, Article 40
1 ball each Yellow Spangle, Green Spangle and Gold & Silver
Spangle. Approximate size: 10 inches in diameter
or
Crochet Cotton, Article 40
1 ball each White, Yellow and Forest Green or colors of your choice
Approximate size: 9 inches in diameter
Crochet hook No. 6
With Green chain (ch) 8, join to form a ring, * ch 12, single crochet
(sc) in ring, repeat from * 6 times, ch 6, double treble crochet ([d tr c]
3 times over hook) in ring (this brings thread in position for next
round), cut Green.

2nd Round. Attach Yellow in any loop, * ch 5, 2 treble crochet (tr c) in 1st stitch (st) of ch, repeat from * once, slip stitch (sl st) in same space with 1st
2 tr c to form petal, * work 2 more petals in same manner, sl st in 1st petal to form group of 3 petals, sc in same loop, ch 5, tr c in 1st st of ch, sc in next loop, ch 5, 2 tr c in 1st st of ch, sl st in center of 3rd petal, ch 5, 2 tr c in 1st st of ch, sl st in base of petal, repeat from * all around ending to correspond and joining last petal to 1st petal, ch 5, tr c in 1st st of ch, join, cut thread.

3rd Round. Attach Gold & Silver Spangle or White in joining and working in back of petals, ch 3, double crochet (dc) in same space, ch 5, 2 dc in next sc, * ch 7, 2 dc in next sc in back of next group of petals, ch 5, 2 dc in next sc in back of same group of petals, repeat from * all around ending with ch 4, tr c in 3rd st of ch.

4th Round. Ch 3, 2 dc in same space, * ch 5, sc in next loop, ch 5, 3 dc in next loop, repeat from * all around ending with ch 5, sc in next loop, ch 5, join in 3rd st of ch.

5th Round. Ch 3, 2 dc in same space, * ch 5, skip next dc, 3 dc in next dc, ch
5, sc in next sc, ch 5, 3 dc in next dc, repeat from * all around, ending to correspond, join in 3rd st of ch.

6th Round. Ch 3, 1 dc in each of the next 2 dc, * ch 5, 3 sc in next loop, ch 5,
1 dc in each of the next 3 dc, sc in next loop, ch 5, sc in next loop, 1 dc in each of the next 3 dc, repeat from * all around ending to correspond, join in
3rd st of ch.

7th Round. Ch 3, 1 dc in each of the next 2 dc, * ch 5, 3 sc in next loop, repeat from * once, ch 5, 1 dc in each of the next 3 dc, sc in next loop, ch 5, sc in same loop, 1 dc in each of the next 3 dc, repeat

from 1st * all around ending to correspond, join in 3rd st of ch.
8th Round. Ch 3, 1 dc in each of the next 2 dc, * ch 5, 3 sc in next loop, repeat from * twice, ch 5, 1 dc in each of the next 3 dc, sc in next loop, 1 dc in each of the next 3 dc, repeat from 1st * all around ending to correspond, join, cut thread.

9th Round. Attach Green in any loop, ch 3, dc in same loop, * ch 5, tr c in
5th st from hook, 2 dc in next loop, repeat from * all around ending with ch
5, tr c in 5th st from hook, join, cut thread.

10th Round. Attach Yellow in same space, ch 8, 2 tr c in 5th st from hook, ch 5, 2 tr c in 5th st from hook, sl st in base of 1st petal, work 2 more petals, sl st in base of 1st petal, * 1 dc in next dc, ch 5, tr c in 5th st from hook, 1 dc in next dc, ch 5, 2 tr c in 5th st from hook, sl st in center of 3rd petal of previous petal group, complete petal and work 2 more petals, sl st in base of 1st petal, repeat from * all around joining 1st and last petals at center and completing round to correspond, cut thread.

11th Round. Attach Gold & Silver Spangle or White in same space and working in back of petal and into dc of round, ch 3, dc in same space, ch 5, 2 dc in next dc, * ch 7, 2 dc in next dc in back of next petal group, ch 5, 2 dc in next dc in back of same petal group, repeat from * all around ending with ch 3, dc in 3rd st of ch.

12th Round. Ch 3, dc in same loop, * ch 5, 2 dc in next loop, repeat from * all around ending with ch 3, dc in 3rd st of ch.
13th Round. Repeat last round.
14th Round. Ch 3, 2 sc in same loop, * 2 sc, ch 3, 2 sc in next loop, repeat from * all around ending with 2 sc in 1st loop, join, cut thread.

The Pineapple Ruffle

Materials Required:
Crochet cotton, Article 40

3 balls White, Cream or Ecru
Approx. Size: 15½ in. diameter without ruffle
or
Crochet Cotton, Article 40
7 balls Silver Spangle or color of your choice
Approximate size: 17½ inches in diameter without ruffle
Crochet hook No. 7
Chain (ch) 4, 11 double crochet (dc) in 4th stitch (st) from hook, join in 3rd st of ch.

2nd Round. * Ch 3, slip stitch (sl st) in next st, repeat from * all around (12 loops).
3rd Round. Sl st into loop, * ch 4, sl st in next loop, repeat from * all around.

4th Round. Sl st into loop, * ch 9, sl st in next loop, repeat from * all around ending with ch 4, double treble crochet ([d tr c] 3 times over hook) in sl st at beginning (this brings thread in position for next round).

5th Round. Ch 3, sc over st just made, * ch 7, 1 sc, ch 3, 1 sc in center st of next large loop, repeat from * all around ending with ch 3, treble crochet (tr c) in d tr c.

6th Round. Same as last round but ending with ch 3, tr c in tr c.
7th Round. Ch 3, sc over tr c, * ch 9, 1 sc, ch 3, 1 sc in center st of next large loop, repeat from * all around ending with ch 4, d tr c in tr c.
8th Round. * Ch 11, sc in next large loop, repeat from * all around, ch 11, join in d tr c.
9th Round. Ch 1, * 6 sc, ch 3, 6 sc in next loop, ch 3, repeat from * all around, join in 1st sc.
10th Round. Sl st to next loop, * ch 7, dc in next loop, ch 7, sl st in next loop, repeat from * all around.

11th Round. Ch 1, * 6 sc in next loop, ch 3, 6 sc in next loop, ch 3, repeat from * all around, join in 1st sc.

12th Round. Sl st to next loop, * ch 8, tr c in next loop, ch 8, sl st in next loop, repeat from * all around.

13th Round. Ch 1, 8 sc in next loop, * ch 3, 8 sc in next loop, sc in next sl st, ch 3, sl st in sc for picot, 8 sc in next loop, repeat from * all around, ending to correspond, join in 1st sc.

14th Round. Sl st to next ch 3 loop, ch 4, 8 tr c in same loop, ch 10, skip the next picot, 7 dc in next ch 3 loop, * ch 10, skip the next picot, 9 tr c in next ch 3 loop, ch 10, skip the next picot, 7 dc in next ch 3 loop, repeat from * all around ending with ch 9, sc in 4th st of ch at beginning.

15th Round. * Ch 3, sc in next tr c, repeat from * 7 times, 5 sc, ch 3, 5 sc in next loop, sc in next dc, * ch 3, sc in next dc, repeat from * 5 times, 5 sc, ch 3, 5 sc in next loop, sc in next tr c, repeat from beginning all around ending last repeat with a sl st in next sc.

16th Round. Sl st into loop, * ch 3, sc in next loop, repeat from * 6 times, ch 5, dc in next ch 3 loop, ch 5, sc in 1st loop of next pineapple, * ch 3, sc in next loop, repeat from * 4 times, ch 5, dc in next ch 3 loop, ch 5, sc in 1st loop of next pineapple, repeat from 1st * all around, join in 1st sl st.

17th Round. Sl st into loop, * ch 3, sc in next loop, repeat from * 5 times, 5 sc in next loop, ch 3, 5 sc in next loop, sc in 1st loop of next pineapple, * ch 3, sc in next loop, repeat from * 3 times, 5 sc in next loop, ch 3, 5 sc in next loop, sc in 1st loop of next pineapple, repeat from 1st * all around, join in sl st.

18th Round. Sl st into loop, * ch 3, sc in next loop, repeat from * 4 times, ch
3, 5 dc in next loop, ch 3, sc in 1st loop of next pineapple, * ch 3, sc in next loop, repeat from * twice, ch 3, 5 dc in next loop, ch 3, sc in 1st loop of next pineapple, repeat from 1st * all around, join in sl st.

19th Round. Sl st into loop, * ch 3, sc in next loop, repeat from * 3 times, ch
3, sc in next dc, ch 3, skip 1 dc, 1 dc, ch 3, 1 dc in next dc, ch 3, skip 1 dc, sc in next dc, ch 3, skip 1 loop, sc in next loop, ch 3, sc in next loop, ch 3, sc in next loop, ch 3, sc in next dc, ch 3, skip 1 dc, 1 dc, ch 3, 1 dc in next dc, ch 3, skip 1 dc, sc in next dc, ch 3, skip 1 loop, sc in next loop, repeat from 1st * all around ending to correspond, join in sl st.

20th Round. Sl st into loop, * ch 3, sc in next loop, repeat from * twice, ch 5, skip 1 loop, 1 sc, ch 3, 1 sc in next loop, * ch 3, 1 sc, ch 3, 1 sc in next loop, repeat from * once, ch 5, skip 1 loop, sc in next loop, ch 3, sc in next loop, ch 5, skip 1 loop, 1 sc, ch 3, 1 sc in next loop, * ch 3, 1 sc, ch 3, 1 sc in next loop, repeat from * once, ch 5, skip 1 loop, sc in next loop, repeat from 1st * all around ending to correspond, join in sl st.

21st Round. Sl st into loop, * ch 3, sc in next loop, ch 3, sc in next loop, ch 9, skip 2 loops, sc in next loop, ch 7, skip 1 loop, sc in next loop, ch 9, skip 2 loops, 1 sc, ch 3, 1 sc in next loop, ch 9, skip 2 loops, sc in next loop, ch 7, skip 1 loop, sc in next loop, ch 9, skip 2 loops, sc in next loop, repeat from * all around ending to correspond, join in sl st.

22nd Round. Sl st into loop, ** ch 5, sl st in 4th st from hook for picot, ch 1, sc in next loop, * ch 9, 1 sc, ch 3, 1 sc in next large loop, repeat from * 5 times, ch 9, sc in 1st loop of next pineapple, repeat from ** all around ending last repeat with ch 4, d tr c in sl st.

Next 3 Rounds. Ch 3, sc over d tr c, * ch 9, 1 sc, ch 3, 1 sc in next large loop, repeat from * all around ending each round with ch 4, d tr c in d tr c.

Next 3 Rounds. Same as last round, but ch 10 for the large loops and end each round with ch 5, d tr c in d tr c.

29th Round. * Ch 11, sc in next large loop, repeat from * all around, ch 11, join in d tr c.

30th Round. Ch 1, * 5 sc, ch 3, 5 sc in next loop, ch 3, repeat from * all around, join in 1st sc.

31st Round. Same as 10th round but ch 6 for each loop.

32nd Round. Same as 11th round but work 5 sc in each loop.

33rd Round. Same as 12th round but ch 7 for each loop.

34th Round. Same as 13th round but work 7 sc in each loop.

Next 3 Rounds. Start ruffle: Work same as 14th, 15th and 16th rounds.

38th Round. Sl st into loop, * ch 3, sc in next loop repeat from * 5 times, ch

5, 1 sc, ch 3, 1 sc in next dc, ch 5, skip 1 loop, sc in next loop, * ch 3, sc in next loop, repeat from * 3 times, ch 5, 1 sc, ch 3, 1 sc in next dc, ch 5, skip 1

loop, sc in next loop, repeat from 1st * all around.

39th Round. Sl st into loop, * ch 3, sc in next loop, repeat from * 4 times, ch

6, skip 1 loop, 1 sc, ch 3, 1 sc, ch 3, 1 sc in next small loop, ch 6, skip 1 loop, sc in 1st loop of next pineapple, * ch 3, sc in next loop, repeat from * twice, ch 6, skip 1 loop, 1 sc, ch 3, 1 sc, ch 3, 1 sc in next small loop, ch 6, skip 1 loop, sc in 1st loop of next pineapple, repeat from 1st * all around ending with a sl st.

40th Round. Sl st into loop, * ch 3, sc in next loop, repeat from * 3 times, ch

6, sc in 5th st of next loop, ch 3, sc in next loop, ch 3, sc in next loop, ch 3, sc in 2nd st of next loop, ch 6, sc in next loop, * ch 3, sc in next loop, repeat from * once, ch 6, sc in 5th st of next loop, ch 3, sc in next loop, ch 3, sc in next loop, ch 3, sc in 2nd st of next loop, ch 6, sc in next loop, repeat from
1st * all around ending with a sl st.

41st Round. Work in the same manner as last round but having 1 more loop in each increasing point and 1 less loop in each pineapple and ch 5 instead of ch 6.

42nd Round. Sl st into loop, ** ch 3, sc in next loop, ch 3, sc in next loop, ch
5, skip 1 loop, sc in next sc, * ch 5, sc in next loop, repeat from * 3 times, ch
5, sc in next sc, ch 5, skip 1 loop, 1 sc, ch 3, 1 sc in next loop, ch 5, skip 1 loop, sc in next sc, * ch 5, sc in next loop, repeat from * 3 times, ch 5, sc in next sc, ch 5, skip 1 loop, sc in next loop, repeat from ** all around ending with a sl st.

43rd Round. Sl st into loop, ** ch 5, sc in 4th st from hook for picot, ch 1, sc in next loop, ch 7, skip 1 loop, sc in next loop, * ch 5, sc in next loop, repeat from * 3 times, ch 7, 1 sc, ch 3, 1 sc in next loop, ch 7, skip next small loop, 1 sc, ch 3, 1 sc in next loop, ch 7, sc in next loop, * ch 5, sc in next loop, repeat from * 3 times, ch 7, skip 1 loop, sc in 1st loop of next pineapple, repeat from ** all around ending last repeat with ch 3, tr c in 1st loop of next pineapple.

44th Round. Ch 3, sc over tr c, ** ch 9, skip next small loop, 1 sc, ch 3, 1 sc in next loop, * ch 7, sc in next loop, repeat from * 4 times, ch 7, skip next small loop, 1 sc, ch 3, 1 sc in next loop, ch 7, skip next small loop, sc in next loop, * ch 7, sc in next loop, repeat from * 3 times, ch 7, 1 sc, ch 3, 1 sc in next loop, repeat from ** all around ending last repeat with ch 3, tr c in tr c.

45th and 46th Rounds. Ch 3, sc over tr c, * ch 8, 1 sc, ch 3, 1 sc in next large loop, repeat from * all around ending each round with ch 4, tr c in tr c.

47th Round. Ch 3, sc over tr c, * ch 8, sl st in 5th st from hook for picot, ch
3, 1 sc, ch 3, 1 sc in next loop, repeat from * all around ending to correspond, join, cut thread.
Small Pineapple Doily

Materials Required:
Crochet cotton, Article 40
2 balls White, Cream, or Ecru
Approximate size: 12 inches in diameter without ruffle
or
Crochet cotton, Article 40
4 balls Silver Spangle or color of your choice
Approximate size: 13½ inches in diameter without ruffle

Crochet hook No. 7

Work 1st 21 rounds same as Pineapple Ruffle Doily.

22nd Round. Sl st into loop, ** ch 5, sl st in 4th st from hook for picot, ch 1, sc in next loop, * ch 7, 1 sc, ch 3, 1 sc in next large loop, repeat from * 5 times, ch 7, sc in next loop, repeat from ** all around ending last repeat with ch 3, tr c in sl st.

Next 3 Rounds. Ch 3, sc over tr c, * ch 7, 1 sc, ch 3, 1 sc in next large loop, repeat from * all around ending each round with ch 3, tr c in tr c.

26th Round. Ch 3, sc over tr c, * ch 8, 1 sc, ch 3, 1 sc in next large loop, repeat from * all around, ending with ch 4, tr c in tr c.

27th Round. * Ch 11, sc in next loop, repeat from * all around ending with ch 11, join in tr c.

28th Round. Ch 4, ** skip 1st st of next loop, dc in next st of same loop, * ch
1, skip next st of same loop, dc in next st of same loop, repeat from * 3 times, ch 1, dc in next sc, ch 1, repeat from ** all around ending to correspond, join in 3rd st of ch.

29th Round. * Ch 7, skip next 2 dc, sc in next dc, repeat from * all around ending with ch 3, tr c in joining.

30th Round. Ch 3, sc over tr c, * ch 7, 1 sc, ch 3, 1 sc in next loop, repeat from * all around ending with ch 3, tr c in tr c.

Next 2 Rounds. Ch 3, sc over tr c, * ch 7, 1 sc, ch 3, 1 sc in next large loop, repeat from * all around ending each round with ch 3, tr c in tr c.

33rd Round. * Ch 8, sc in next large loop, repeat from * all around, ch 8, join in tr c.

34th Round. Ch 1, * 4 sc, ch 3, 4 sc in next loop, ch 3, repeat from * all around ending last repeat with ch 1, sc in 1st sc.

35th Round. Ch 7, sl st in next loop, * ch 4, dc in next loop, ch 4, sl st in next loop, repeat from * all around, ch 4, join in 3rd st of ch.

36th Round. Ch 1, * 4 sc in next loop, ch 3, 4 sc in next loop, ch 3, repeat from * all around ending last repeat with ch 1, sc in 1st sc.
37th Round. * Ch 5, tr c in next loop, ch 5, sl st in next loop, repeat from * all around.

38th Round. Ch 3, sl st in same space for picot, * 5 sc, in next loop, sc in next tr c, ch 3, sl st in sc just made for picot, 5 sc in next loop, sc in next sl st, ch 3, sl st in sc just made for picot, repeat from * all around ending to correspond, join, cut thread.

DIRECTIONS FOR STARCHING DOILIES

Starch: Dissolve ½ cup starch in ½ cup of cold water. Boil about 1¼ cups of water, remove from flame, then slowly stir the starch mixture into boiling water, stirring constantly. Place back on flame until it thickens.

As soon as starch is cool enough to handle, dip doily and squeeze starch through it thoroughly. Wring out extra starch. The doily should be wet with starch but there should be none in the spaces. Pin center of doily in position according to size and leave until thoroughly dry. If steam iron is used, iron ruffles after it is dry. If regular iron is used, dampen ruffle slightly before pressing. Pin folds of ruffle in position and leave until thoroughly dry.

18051274R00058